Betty Crocker's GOOD AND EASY COOKBOOK

Photography Directors:
LEN WEISS / STEPHEN MANVILLE

 **GOLDEN PRESS • NEW YORK**
Western Publishing Company, Inc.
Racine, Wisconsin

REVISED EDITION
with recipes selected from the original edition

First Printing This Format, 1980

Library of Congress Catalog Card Number: 76–150742

To Busy Cooks Everywhere—

Good and easy. It's an unbeatable combination of the best of both worlds. And with this cookbook in hand, you can prepare 365 breakfasts, lunches and dinners every year, in a hurry—without skimping on quality or any of the nice little touches that make mealtime a pleasure.

Consider this latest edition of *Good and Easy* your ultra-modern shortcut to this kind of mealtime pleasure. We show you how to use convenience foods in new and unusual ways; how to serve nourishing food without being ho-hum; how to plan menus that will make your family sit up and take notice. We offer ingredient substitutions to help you use what you have on hand. We suggest splendid revivals for leftovers. And for instant decision-making, we have main-meal meats at the beginning—because they're the starting point for most of your meal planning.

We hope you'll use these recipes as guides to branch out and create ideas of your own—that's part of the fun of cooking. And we'd like to think that our *Good and Easy Cookbook* will give you extra time for the many other good things in your life.

Cordially,

P.S. Each and every recipe has been tested, of course—in our Kitchens and in the kitchens of busy cooks across the country.

Contents

Pictured at right:

TOP
Orange-glazed Baked Ham
    Skillet-glazed Sweet Potatoes
Herbed Salmon Steaks
Golden Parmesan Chicken

CENTER
Polish Sausage Boil
Country Cassoulet
Mixed Grill

BOTTOM
Meatball Stew
Breaded Veal Cutlets
Braised Short Ribs

Meats and Main Dishes

Stop! Here's where the road to good and easy mealtimes begins. You probably start thinking about the meat you're going to serve for dinner first. Right? Well, we do too. Why? Because until that decision has been made, you can't even begin to think intelligently about side dishes and desserts. And besides, you'll have a much better idea of what you can do with the rest of the food budget. It only stands to reason, then, that the main-meal meat becomes the natural starting point for your over-all menu plot, be it daily or weekly.

So choose your entree from this chapter—depending on the week's best buys, or what you have in the freezer. Then move on to the following chapters and round out the three daily meals—remembering snacktime, of course. You'll find some interesting menu clues with many of these main dish recipes. (And if you feel you need to brush up on the basics of meal planning, take our refresher course on pages 120 and 121.)

Be Choosy

Eye those meat cuts like a pro. Look for flecks of fat within the lean; it's called marbling, and in moderate amounts it increases juiciness, flavor and tenderness. Take note of the U.S. stamp of approval, too, which tells you all is well. And where grading is concerned, remember this: U.S. Prime and Choice offer quality but the less expensive grades, if properly cooked, give you the same good nutrition.

Be bright about bargains. Ask questions about the day's best buys. If your meat retailer has a special on a new cut, go ahead and try it—for variety and savings. When you spot a particularly good buy on roast beef, for example, think ahead: Sunday's dinner, Tuesday's casserole. Then buy for two meals at a time and plan to combine the leftovers with speedy, easy convenience foods. Take a clue from Savory Beef Pie (page 14). If you're not looking to

"planned overs," buy in exact amounts. Meat that you don't need or won't eat is an expensive loss.

How Much Is Enough?

As a rule of thumb, figure on 3 ounces of *cooked* meat or 4 ounces of *uncooked* meat for each serving. Here are some guidelines to follow:

Meats with large bone	1 or 1½ servings per pound
Meats with medium bone (pot-roast, ham, chicken, rib roast, dressed fish)	2 or 3 servings per pound
Meats with small or no bone (ground meat, fish fillets, boneless roast)	3 or 4 servings per pound

With main dish combinations like Dried Beef Casserole (page 14), however, the meat protein is supplemented by that of other foods; so you can get by with less meat.

Storing Meat

Store fresh meat uncovered or loosely covered in the coldest part of the refrigerator. Keep the temperature as low as possible without actually freezing the meat. Plan on using fresh meats within 2 or 3 days, ground meats and variety meats within 24 hours. Cured or smoked meats can be stored 1 to 2 weeks.

Take special care with cooked meats and casseroles. Cool *quickly*, then cover or wrap tightly; they, too, go in coldest part of the refrigerator. You can speed the cooling of a main dish casserole by placing it in a pan of ice and water.

And lucky you, if you own a freezer. You can really shop and cook for the good and easy life. See pages 122-123 for specific information for freezing and thawing meats and main dishes.

Beef

TO ROAST BEEF

Select roast from those listed in chart below. Allow about ½ pound per person—less for boneless roasts, more for roasts with a bone. If desired, season with salt and pepper before, during or after roasting.

Place meat fat side up on rack in open shallow roasting pan. The rack keeps the meat out of the drippings. (In roasts such as standing rib, the ribs form a natural rack.) It is not necessary to baste.

Insert meat thermometer so tip is in center of thickest part of meat and does not touch bone or rest in fat. Do not add water. Do not cover.

Roast meat in 325° oven. (It is not necessary to preheat oven.) Roast to desired degree of doneness (see Timetable), using thermometer reading as final guide.

Roasts are easier to carve if allowed to set 15 to 20 minutes after removing from oven. Since meat continues to cook after removal from oven, if roast is to "set," it should be removed from oven when the thermometer registers 5 to 10° lower than the desired doneness.

You'll fine some guidelines for carving a standing rib roast on page 124.

HORSERADISH SAUCE

In chilled bowl, beat ½ cup chilled whipping cream until stiff; stir in 3 tablespoons horseradish and ½ teaspoon salt. Refrigerate until serving time.

1 cup.

TIMETABLE

Cut	Approximate Weight	Meat Thermometer Reading	Approximate Cooking Time (Minutes per Pound)
Rib	6 to 8 pounds	140° (rare) 160° (medium) 170° (well)	23 to 25 27 to 30 32 to 35
	4 to 6 pounds	140° (rare) 160° (medium) 170° (well)	26 to 32 34 to 38 40 to 42
Boneless Rib	5 to 7 pounds	140° (rare) 160° (medium) 170° (well)	32 38 48
Rib Eye (Delmonico)*	4 to 6 pounds	140° (rare) 160° (medium) 170° (well)	18 to 20 20 to 22 22 to 24
Rolled Rump (high quality)	4 to 6 pounds	150 to 170°	25 to 30
Tip (high quality)	3½ to 4 pounds	140 to 170°	35 to 40
Tenderloin (whole)**	4 to 6 pounds	140° (rare)	45 to 60 minutes (total)
Tenderloin (half)**	2 to 3 pounds	140° (rare)	45 to 50 minutes (total)

*Roast at 350°   **Roast at 425°

CALIFORNIA ROAST

4-pound beef rolled rump roast
1 cup orange juice
1 cup tomato juice
¼ cup salad oil
2 teaspoons salt
½ teaspoon allspice
¼ teaspoon chili powder
⅛ teaspoon instant minced garlic
 Tangy California Gravy (below)

Place meat in deep glass bowl or plastic bag. Mix remaining ingredients except Tangy California Gravy; pour on meat. Cover; refrigerate at least 4 hours, turning meat occasionally. Remove meat from marinade; reserve 2 cups of the marinade for the gravy.

Place meat fat side up on rack in open shallow roasting pan. Insert meat thermometer so tip is in center of thickest part of meat and does not rest in fat. Roast in 325° oven to desired degree of doneness, about 2 hours. (Meat thermometer should register 150° for rare, 160° for medium, 170° for well.) Place meat on warm platter; keep warm while making gravy.

8 to 10 servings.

TANGY CALIFORNIA GRAVY

Heat reserved marinade to boiling. In tightly covered jar, shake ¼ cup water, 2 tablespoons vinegar and 3 tablespoons flour; stir into hot marinade. (If you prefer a less tangy gravy, omit vinegar and shake flour with ⅓ cup water.) Heat to boiling, stirring constantly. Boil and stir 1 minute. If necessary, season with salt and pepper.

To Cook on a Rotisserie: Insert spit rod lengthwise through center of roast; secure with holding forks. Check balance by rotating spit in palms of hands. Insert meat thermometer in center of thickest part of meat, making sure it does not touch fat or spit. Set oven control to rotisserie. Cook roast until thermometer registers 5 to 10° below desired doneness, about 2 hours.

Substitutions

For rolled rump roast: 4-pound beef tip roast.
For instant garlic: 1 clove garlic, minced.

CRANBERRY-PEPPER ROAST

4-pound beef tip roast
2 tablespoons cracked pepper
3 tablespoons salad oil
2⅔ cups cranberry cocktail
 Cranberry Gravy (below)

Score meat (cut lightly in a crisscross pattern). Rub all sides but not ends with pepper. Brown meat in oil over medium heat, about 15 minutes.

Reduce heat; pour cranberry cocktail on meat. Cover tightly; simmer on top of range or in 325° oven 2½ hours or until tender. Place meat on warm platter; keep warm while making gravy.

8 servings.

CRANBERRY GRAVY

Strain hot broth; measure 3 cups and heat to boiling. In tightly covered jar, shake ¾ cup cranberry cocktail and ⅓ cup all-purpose flour; stir into hot liquid. Heat to boiling, stirring constantly. Boil and stir 1 minute. Season with salt.

Substitutions

For tip roast: 4-pound beef rolled rump roast.
For cranberry cocktail: 2⅔ cups water with the roast and ¾ cup water in the gravy.

POT-ROAST IN FOIL

4-pound beef chuck pot-roast
1 envelope (about 1½ ounces)
 onion soup mix
1 can (10¾ ounces) condensed cream of
 mushroom soup

Place 30 × 18-inch piece of heavy-duty aluminum foil in baking pan, 13 × 9 × 2 inches; place meat on foil. Sprinkle soup mix on meat and spread with cream of mushroom soup. Fold foil over meat and seal securely. Cook in 300° oven 4 hours.

Menu-mate: Orange-Cauliflower Salad (page 56).

8 to 10 servings.

Substitution

For chuck pot-roast: 4-pound beef rump, top round or bottom round roast.

TO BROIL BEEF

For each serving, allow about 1 pound of any steak with a bone, about ½ pound for boneless cuts.

Diagonally slash outer edge of fat on steak at 1-inch intervals to prevent curling (do not cut into lean). Set oven control at broil and/or 550°. Place meat on rack in broiler pan so tops of ¾- to 1-inch steaks are 2 to 3 inches from heat, 1- to 2-inch steaks are 3 to 5 inches from heat. Broil until brown. The meat should be about half done (see Timetable).

If desired, season brown side with salt and pepper. (Always season after browning as salt tends to draw moisture to surface and delay browning.) Turn meat; broil until brown.

TIMETABLE

Cut	Approximate Cooking Time per Side	
	Rare	Medium
Rib, Rib Eye or Top Loin Steak		
1 inch	8 minutes	10 minutes
1½ inches	12 minutes	15 minutes
2 inches	17 minutes	22 minutes
Sirloin, Porterhouse or T-bone Steak		
1 inch	10 minutes	12 minutes
1½ inches	15 minutes	17 minutes
Tenderloin (Filet Mignon)		
(4 to 8 ounces)	5 to 7 minutes	8 to 10 minutes
Chuck Eye Steak (high quality)		
1 inch	12 minutes	15 minutes
1½ inches	20 minutes	22 minutes
Ground Beef Patties		
(1 inch)	7 minutes	12 minutes

TERIYAKI STEAK

    2-pound beef sirloin steak,
        1 to 1¼ inches thick
    ½ cup soy sauce
    ½ cup water
    1 tablespoon brown sugar
    1½ teaspoons ginger

Diagonally slash outer edge of fat on steak at 1-inch intervals to prevent curling (do not cut into lean). Score meat (cut lightly in a crisscross pattern) and place in shallow glass dish. Heat remaining ingredients to boiling, stirring occasionally; pour on meat. Cover; refrigerate at least 2 hours, turning meat occasionally.

Set oven control at broil and/or 550°. Remove meat from marinade. Broil 3 to 4 inches from heat about 10 minutes on each side for rare, about 12 minutes for medium. Cut meat across grain at a slanted angle into ¼-inch slices.

Play up the Oriental origin and serve with Snow Peas and Carrot Nuggets (page 62), buttered rice and, as dessert, lemon sherbet and Polynesian Cookies (page 91).

8 servings.

Substitution

For sirloin steak: 2 pounds beef round steak, ¾ inch thick; broil 8 minutes for medium, 10 minutes for well.

Charcoal-grilled Steak

Whether you're splurging with sirloin or going the way of a round steak and meat tenderizer, you'll want to do it right. So choose steaks 1 to 2 inches thick. Trim off excess fat (to cut down on flare-ups). Slash rest of fat every 2 inches; this keeps steak from curling. Check timetable below; check coals to be sure they're hot. (If you can hold your hand near the grid 3 seconds, they're *not*!) When you're ready to go, grill steaks 4 inches from coals; use tongs to turn. Season after turning and after grilling. To test for doneness, make a knife slit along the bone.

	1 Inch Thick Minutes per Side	2 Inches Thick Minutes per Side
Rare	4 to 5	12 to 13
Medium	7 to 8	15 to 17
Well	10 to 11	22 to 25

PEPPER STEAK BORDELAISE

1½ pounds sirloin steak, ½ inch thick
2 tablespoons salad oil
½ teaspoon salt
½ teaspoon freshly ground pepper
1 clove garlic, minced
1 green pepper, cut into 1-inch pieces (about 1 cup)
1 can (13¼ ounces) Bordelaise sauce
2 tomatoes, peeled and cut into eighths
3 to 4 cups hot cooked rice

Trim fat and bone from meat; cut into 4 to 6 serving pieces. In large skillet, brown meat on one side in oil over medium-high heat. Turn meat; season with ¼ teaspoon salt and ¼ teaspoon pepper. Brown other side of meat; turn. Season with remaining salt and pepper. Remove meat from skillet.

In same skillet, cook and stir garlic and green pepper until tender. Stir in Bordelaise sauce. Add meat; cook uncovered 10 minutes. Add tomatoes; heat through. Serve on rice.

Orange and Onion Salad (page 56) is a colorful companion.

4 to 6 servings.

BARBECUED ROUND STEAK

2-pound beef round steak, ¾ inch thick
2 tablespoons salad oil
3 tablespoons instant chopped onion
1 cup barbecue sauce
½ cup water

Cut meat into 6 serving pieces. In large skillet or Dutch oven, brown meat in oil over medium heat. Stir in remaining ingredients. Cover tightly; cook on top of range or in 325° oven 1½ hours or until meat is tender.

Suggested accompaniments: green beans, Carrots Bouillon (page 60) and Ambrosia Salad (page 56).

6 servings.

Substitutions

For round steak: 2-pound beef tip steak.
For instant onion: ½ cup chopped onion.

STEAK SUPPER IN FOIL

1½-pound chuck steak, 1 inch thick
1 can (10¾ ounces) condensed cream of mushroom soup
1 envelope (about 1½ ounces) onion soup mix
3 medium carrots, quartered
2 stalks celery, cut into 2-inch pieces
3 medium potatoes, pared and quartered
2 tablespoons water

Heat oven to 450°. Place 24 × 18-inch piece of heavy-duty aluminum foil in baking pan; place meat on foil. Stir together mushroom soup and onion soup mix (dry); spread on meat. Top meat with vegetables; sprinkle water on vegetables. Fold foil over and seal securely. Cook 1½ hours or until tender.

All this meal needs is the zing of Country-style Waldorf Salad (page 56). For dessert, serve ice cream and Brownies (page 88).

4 servings.

CUBE STEAK STROGANOFF

1 package (about 17½ ounces) beef cubed steaks
1 package (5.25 ounces) noodles Stroganoff
¼ teaspoon garlic salt
⅛ teaspoon pepper
   Sliced pitted ripe olives
   Pimiento strips

Cut meat into ½-inch strips. Brown meat over medium-high heat. Drain off fat; set meat aside. Cook noodles Stroganoff as directed on package. Stir in meat, garlic salt and pepper. Garnish with olive slices and pimiento strips.

Company fare with Asparagus à la Polonaise (page 58), Sweet and Sour Beets (page 59) and Orange-Cherry Pie (page 84).

4 servings.

Pictured at right:
Steak Supper in Foil—a one-dish dinner
that's tailor-made for today.

SWISS STEAK

¼ cup all-purpose flour
½ teaspoon salt
¼ teaspoon pepper
2-pound beef round steak, 1 inch thick
2 tablespoons shortening
1 can (8 ounces) tomatoes
½ cup minced onion
¼ cup minced green pepper
½ teaspoon salt
⅛ teaspoon pepper

Mix flour, salt and pepper. Sprinkle one side of meat with half the flour mixture; pound in. Turn meat; pound in remaining flour mixture. Cut meat into 6 serving pieces. Melt shortening in large skillet; add meat and brown over medium heat, about 15 minutes.

Cover tightly; simmer 1 hour. Add small amount of water if necessary. Mix remaining ingredients; pour on meat. Cover tightly; simmer 30 minutes or until tender.

Broccoli 'n Chips (page 60), combining two family favorites, is a good choice for the vegetable.

6 servings.

Substitutions

For round steak: 2-pound beef tip steak.
For fresh onion: 3 tablespoons instant minced onion.
For fresh green pepper: 2 tablespoons dried green pepper.

LONDON BROIL

Score 1½- to 2-pound flank steak; place in shallow glass dish. Pour 1 bottle (8 ounces) Italian salad dressing on steak. Cover; refrigerate at least 8 hours, turning meat occasionally.

Set oven control at broil and/or 550°. Remove steak from dressing; reserve dressing. Broil steak 3 to 4 inches from heat about 5 minutes on each side, brushing several times with the reserved dressing. Cut meat across grain at a slanted angle into thin slices.

4 to 6 servings.

BRAISED SHORT RIBS

Pictured on page 5.

2 pounds beef short ribs, cut into pieces
2 teaspoons salt
½ teaspoon pepper
2 tablespoons shortening
½ cup water
2 tablespoons horseradish
8 small carrots
4 medium onions
3 stalks celery, cut into eighths

Season meat with salt and pepper. Melt shortening in Dutch oven; brown meat over medium-high heat. Drain off fat. Pour water and horseradish on meat.

Cover tightly; simmer on top of range or in 325° oven about 2½ hours or until meat is tender. Add small amount of water if necessary. About 1 hour before end of cooking time, add vegetables.

Nice with fluffy mashed potatoes and Tossed Salad with Classic Dressing (page 53).

4 servings.

BEEF MUSHROOM

1 pound beef stew meat, cut into 1-inch cubes
½ teaspoon seasoned instant meat tenderizer
2 tablespoons salad oil
1 can (10½ ounces) mushroom gravy
5 ounces uncooked medium noodles

Sprinkle meat with tenderizer; pierce each piece with fork. Cover; refrigerate 2 to 24 hours.

In large skillet, brown meat in oil over medium heat. Reduce heat; stir in gravy. Cover tightly; simmer about 45 minutes, stirring occasionally. (Meat will not be fork-tender but it will be tender to eat.)

Cook noodles as directed on package; drain. Serve beef and gravy on noodles.

Complete the meal with Green and Gold Salad (page 54) and Biscuit Fan-tans (page 70). And for dessert, offer Caramel Peach Crisps (page 94).

3 or 4 servings.

GOOD BROWN STEW

2 pounds beef stew meat, cut into
  1-inch cubes
1 to 2 tablespoons salad oil
¼ cup instant chopped onion
1 small bay leaf
2 teaspoons salt
1 teaspoon sugar
¼ teaspoon allspice
⅛ teaspoon instant minced garlic
1 teaspoon lemon juice
1 teaspoon Worcestershire sauce
1 can (16 ounces) whole carrots, drained
  (reserve liquid)
1 can (15 ounces) whole potatoes, drained
  (reserve liquid)
1 can (8 ounces) whole onions, drained
  (reserve liquid)

In Dutch oven, brown meat in oil over medium heat. Sprinkle seasonings on meat. Add enough water to reserved vegetable liquids to measure 4 cups; pour on meat. Heat to boiling.

Reduce heat; simmer 2 hours or until meat is tender. Add small amount of water if necessary. Add vegetables; simmer 15 minutes longer or until vegetables are heated through.

Serve with a simple salad of lettuce wedges and a typical U.S.A. dessert—strawberry shortcake.

6 servings.

Substitutions

For instant onion: 1 large onion, chopped.
For instant garlic: 1 clove garlic, minced.
For canned vegetables: 6 carrots, quartered, 3 medium potatoes, pared and cut into eighths, 8 small onions; add 30 minutes before end of cooking time.

Stew-pendous Substitutes

You're proud of your beef stew and you always buy foreshank or brisket beef. But why not branch out? Especially if you find a special on beef. From the chuck, use blade or arm pot-roast. From the round, use rump or round roast; the steaks, too. For a lighter stew, switch off to veal or lamb—just forego the browning.

OVEN STEW

2 pounds beef round steak, cut into
  1-inch cubes
2 cups sliced carrots
1 cup sliced celery
2 medium onions, sliced
1 can (5 ounces) water chestnuts,
  drained and sliced
1 can (6 ounces) sliced mushrooms, drained
3 tablespoons flour
1 tablespoon sugar
1 tablespoon salt
1 can (16 ounces) tomatoes
1 cup red Burgundy

Mix meat, carrots, celery, onions, water chestnuts and mushrooms in Dutch oven. Mix flour, sugar and salt; stir into meat mixture. Stir in tomatoes and wine. Cover tightly; cook in 325° oven or on top of range 4 hours.

Bread in the Round (page 71) goes well with this easy but elegant stew.

6 servings.

Substitution

For Burgundy: 1 cup water and 1 teaspoon instant beef bouillon.

PICCALILLI STEW

1 can (24 ounces) beef stew
½ cup pickle relish

Stir together stew and pickle relish in saucepan. Simmer about 10 minutes or until heated through.

Quick meal plan: sliced tomatoes, bread sticks and a fixed-up frozen apple pie (page 83).

4 servings.

VARIATION

■ *Stroganoff Stew:* Stir ½ cup dairy sour cream into heated stew, or serve sour cream as a garnish. Nice to serve on toast.

SAVORY BEEF PIE

> 2 tablespoons shortening
> ¼ cup chopped onion
> 2 tablespoons chopped green pepper
> 2 cups cut-up cooked beef
> 2 cups cooked vegetables
> 1¼ cups gravy
> Drop Biscuits

Melt shortening in large skillet; cook and stir onion and green pepper until tender. Stir in meat, vegetables and gravy; heat about 5 minutes.

Heat oven to 450°. Prepare 10 to 12 Drop Biscuits as directed on buttermilk baking mix package except—drop dough by spoonfuls onto hot meat mixture. Bake uncovered 15 to 20 minutes or until biscuits are brown.

Serve with individual tossed green salads and, for the finale, Double Fudge Cake (page 77).

4 to 6 servings.

Substitutions

For gravy: 1 can (10¾ ounces) gravy or 1 envelope (⅞ ounce) gravy mix prepared as directed.

For cooked vegetables: 1 package (10 ounces) frozen mixed vegetables, broken apart.

VARIATIONS

■ *Savory Lamb or Veal Pie:* Substitute 2 cups cut-up cooked lamb or veal for the beef.

Spicing Up Yesterday's Beef

Sunday dinner's gone, but the pot-roast lingers on. Lucky you, you're a meal ahead. And here's your chance to experiment with spices. Accompany the second go-round with fluffy mashed potatoes and whip in a taste of horseradish and a pinch of dill weed. Delicious! Or how about beefing up the leftover gravy with a dash of allspice or nutmeg?

If cold beef sandwiches are a specialty of the house, spice up the spread for the bread—just a sprinkling of chili powder or ginger mixed into the butter.

For a salad supper, try this: diced cold beef and rice, mixed with mayonnaise and spiced with dill weed, mace or soy sauce.

However and whatever you spice, sprinkle softly. You know what they say about too much of a good thing.

DRIED BEEF CASSEROLE

> 1 cup uncooked elbow macaroni
>   (about 4 ounces)
> 1 can (10¾ ounces) condensed cream
>   of mushroom soup
> ½ cup milk
> 1 cup shredded Cheddar cheese
>   (about 4 ounces)
> 3 tablespoons finely chopped onion
> ¼ pound dried beef,* cut into
>   bite-size pieces
> 2 hard-cooked eggs, sliced

Heat oven to 350°. Cook macaroni as directed on package; drain. Blend soup and milk in large bowl. Stir in cheese, onion, macaroni and dried beef; fold in eggs.

Pour mixture into ungreased 1½-quart casserole. Cover tightly; bake 30 minutes or until heated through.

4 to 6 servings.

*If dried beef is very salty, pour boiling water over it and drain.

Substitution

For fresh onion: 1 tablespoon instant minced onion.

CORNED BEEF STEW

> 1 can (12 ounces) corned beef
> 1 can (15 ounces) sliced white potatoes,
>   drained
> 1 can (16 ounces) tomatoes, cut up
> 1 can (16 ounces) whole onions
> 1 package (10 ounces) frozen peas and
>   carrots
> 1 teaspoon salt
> ½ teaspoon marjoram
> ½ teaspoon thyme
> 2 cups shredded Cheddar cheese
>   (8 ounces)

Break apart corned beef in Dutch oven. Stir in potatoes, tomatoes (with liquid), onions (with liquid), frozen peas and carrots, salt, marjoram and thyme. Heat to boiling, stirring occasionally. Reduce heat. Cover tightly; simmer 30 minutes. Serve topped with cheese.

6 servings.

LIVER

To Panfry: Have liver sliced ½ to ¾ inch thick. Coat with flour. Melt ¼ cup shortening in skillet; brown liver over medium-high heat, 2 to 3 minutes on each side. Season to taste.

To Broil: Have baby beef, veal (calf) or lamb liver sliced ½ to ¾ inch thick. Dip into melted bacon drippings, butter or margarine. Set oven control at broil and/or 550°. Broil liver 3 to 5 inches from heat just long enough for meat to change color and become light brown, about 3 minutes on each side.

To Braise: Have beef or pork liver sliced ½ to ¾ inch thick. Coat with flour. Brown in small amount of fat. Add ¼ cup liquid. Cover tightly; cook on top of range or in 350° oven 20 to 30 minutes. For a large piece, increase liquid to ½ cup; cook about 30 minutes per pound.

LIVER AND ONIONS

Have 1 pound liver sliced ½ to ¾ inch thick. In large skillet, cook and stir 2 cups thinly sliced onion in 3 tablespoons butter or margarine until tender. Remove from skillet; keep warm. Panfry liver as directed above. Add onions for the last minute of cooking.

4 servings.

LIVER CREOLE

    4 slices bacon
    1 pound sliced beef liver
    3 tablespoons flour
    ⅓ cup chopped green pepper
    1 can (16 ounces) tomatoes
1½ teaspoons salt
    ½ teaspoon chili powder
    ⅛ teaspoon cayenne red pepper

Fry bacon until crisp; remove bacon and drain. Drain off all but 3 tablespoons fat. Coat liver with flour; brown in bacon fat. Stir in remaining ingredients except bacon. Cover tightly; simmer 20 minutes. Garnish with bacon.

4 servings.

Liver and Onions

Liver Creole

BAKED MEATBALLS

2 pounds ground beef
1 cup dry bread crumbs
½ cup milk
2 eggs
¼ cup instant minced onion
2 teaspoons salt
¼ teaspoon pepper

Mix all ingredients. Shape mixture by ¼ cupfuls into balls (do not pack). Place in ungreased jelly roll pan, 15½ × 10½ × 1 inch. Bake uncovered in 350° oven 30 to 40 minutes or until brown.

6 servings (18 meatballs).

Substitutions

For dry bread crumbs: 3 slices bread, cubed.
For instant onion: ¾ cup minced onion.

MEATBALL STEW

Pictured on page 5.

1 pound ground beef
1 egg
½ cup dry bread crumbs
¼ cup milk
2 tablespoons instant minced onion
1 teaspoon salt
⅛ teaspoon pepper
1 can (16 ounces) stewed tomatoes
1 package (24 ounces) frozen vegetables for stew
2 teaspoons salt

Mix ground beef, egg, bread crumbs, milk, onion, 1 teaspoon salt and the pepper. Shape mixture by ¼ cupfuls into balls (do not pack); brown in Dutch oven over medium-high heat. Drain off fat.

Stir in stewed tomatoes, frozen vegetables and 2 teaspoons salt; heat to boiling. Reduce heat. Cover tightly; simmer on top of range or in 325° oven until vegetables are tender, 1¼ to 1½ hours.

Serve with Garlic French Bread Sticks (page 68) and, for dessert, Spice Cake with Browned Butter Icing (page 79).

4 or 5 servings.

Substitution

For instant onion: ⅓ cup minced onion.

BAKED MEAT LOAF

2 pounds ground beef
1 cup seasoned bread crumbs
¾ cup milk
2 eggs
2 tablespoons instant minced onion
2 teaspoons salt
¼ teaspoon pepper

Mix all ingredients. Spread mixture in ungreased loaf pan, 9 × 5 × 3 inches. Bake uncovered in 350° oven about 1½ hours or until done.

8 to 10 servings.

Substitution

For instant onion: ¼ cup minced onion.

CORN HAMBURGER BAKE

1 pound ground beef
1 large onion, sliced
¼ cup sliced celery
2 cans (16 ounces each) cream-style corn
1 teaspoon salt
¼ teaspoon pepper
1 teaspoon instant beef bouillon
1 cup buttermilk baking mix
2 tablespoons butter or margarine, melted
¼ teaspoon garlic salt

Heat oven to 450°. Cook and stir ground beef, onion and celery in large skillet until meat is brown. Drain off fat.

Reserve ½ cup of the corn. Stir remaining corn, the salt, pepper and instant bouillon into meat mixture; heat to boiling. Pour into ungreased 2½-quart casserole.

Stir baking mix and reserved corn with fork to a soft dough. Drop dough by tablespoonfuls onto hot meat mixture. Mix butter and garlic salt; drizzle half the butter on biscuit dough. Bake 20 to 25 minutes. Brush biscuits with remaining butter.

For the salad, offer lettuce with a simple dressing of mayonnaise laced with chili sauce or turn to your favorite combination of mixed greens.

6 servings.

Substitution

For instant bouillon: 1 beef bouillon cube.

COMPLETE HAMBURGER CASSEROLE

1 pound ground beef
1 tablespoon instant minced onion
½ teaspoon salt
½ teaspoon pepper
1 package (10 ounces) frozen mixed
 vegetables, broken apart
1 can (11 ounces) condensed Cheddar
 cheese soup
1 package (16 ounces) frozen fried
 shredded potato rounds

Heat oven to 375°. Mix beef, onion, salt and pepper in ungreased 2-quart casserole. Arrange vegetables on meat; pour cheese soup on vegetables. Cover with frozen potato rounds. Bake uncovered 1 hour or until potatoes are golden brown.

Add crunch to this dinner in a dish with celery and carrot sticks. Try Raspberry-Raspberry (page 95) and Almond Shortbreads (page 89) for dessert.

4 or 5 servings.

Substitutions

For instant onion: 3 tablespoons minced onion.
For frozen mixed vegetables: 1 package (10 ounces) frozen peas and carrots, corn or chopped broccoli.
For cheese soup: 1 cup cheese sauce.

HEARTY HAMBURGER BAKE

1 pound ground beef
1 small onion, chopped (about ⅓ cup)
1 teaspoon salt
¼ teaspoon pepper
1 can (16 ounces) cut green beans, drained
1 can (10¾ ounces) condensed tomato
 soup
 Instant mashed potatoes (enough
 for 4 servings)

Heat oven to 350°. Cook and stir meat and onion in large skillet until meat is brown. Drain off fat. Stir in seasonings, beans and soup. Pour into ungreased 2-quart casserole.

Prepare mashed potatoes as directed on package. Spoon potatoes onto meat mixture in 4 mounds. Bake uncovered 30 minutes or until bubbly.

4 servings.

COUNTRY-STYLE HOMINY

1 pound ground beef
¼ cup instant chopped onion
⅛ teaspoon instant minced garlic
⅓ cup chopped ripe or pimiento-stuffed
 olives
1 can (28 ounces) tomatoes
1 teaspoon salt
1 teaspoon oregano
⅛ teaspoon red pepper sauce
¼ cup butter or margarine
2 cans (20 ounces each) hominy, drained

Cook and stir ground beef, onion and garlic until meat is brown. Drain off fat. Stir in remaining ingredients except butter and hominy. Simmer uncovered 1 hour.

Melt butter in medium saucepan. Stir hominy into butter; heat through. Serve sauce on hominy.

4 to 6 servings.

Substitutions

For instant onion: 1 large onion, chopped.
For instant garlic: 1 clove garlic, minced.
For hominy: 3 to 4 cups hot cooked rice, macaroni or noodles.

HAMBURGER STROGANOFF

1 pound ground beef
½ cup minced onion
1 clove garlic, minced
1 can (10¾ ounces) condensed cream of
 mushroom soup
1 teaspoon salt
1 cup dairy sour cream
2 to 3 cups hot cooked noodles

Cook and stir ground beef, onion and garlic until meat is brown. Stir in mushroom soup and salt; simmer uncovered 10 minutes. Mix in sour cream; heat through. Serve on noodles.

4 servings.

Substitutions

For fresh onion: 3 tablespoons instant minced onion.
For garlic clove: ⅛ teaspoon instant minced garlic.

Chili Con Carne

Giant Burger

CHILI CON CARNE

  1 **pound ground beef**
  ½ **pound bulk pork sausage**
  1 **can (16 ounces) tomatoes**
  1 **can (15½ ounces) chili beans**
  4 **medium onions, chopped (about 2 cups)**

In large skillet, cook and stir ground beef and pork sausage until brown. Drain off fat. Stir in remaining ingredients; simmer uncovered 1 hour.

Nice with Molded Waldorf Salad (page 55) and crackers or quick-from-a-mix corn muffins.

4 servings.

Substitution

    For chili beans: 1 can (15½ ounces) kidney beans and 1 to 2 tablespoons chili powder.

GIANT BURGER

1½ **pounds ground beef**
1½ **teaspoons salt**
  1 **package (3 ounces) cream cheese, softened**
  1 **tablespoon prepared mustard**
  1 **tablespoon horseradish, drained**
  1 **can (3 ounces) French fried onions, if desired**

Heat oven to 350°. Mix ground beef and salt; divide in half. Pat one half evenly in 8-inch pie pan. Mix cream cheese, mustard and horseradish; spread to within 1 inch of edge of meat in pan.

Shape remaining meat into 8-inch circle. Place on cheese mixture; pinch edge to seal securely. Bake uncovered 45 minutes for medium, 55 minutes for well.

Heat onions in oven 5 minutes. Remove meat to large serving plate; arrange onions around meat. Cut into wedges.

Complete menu plan: Mushroom Italian Green Beans (page 59), Cucumber Relish Mold (page 55), potatoes and Caramel Peach Crisps (page 94).

4 to 6 servings.

VARIATION

■ *Gourmet Burger:* Add 2 tablespoons crumbled blue cheese to cream cheese mixture.

Pork

TO ROAST FRESH PORK

Select roast from those listed in chart below. Allow about ½ pound per person—less for boneless roasts, more for roasts with a bone. If desired, season with salt and pepper.

Place meat fat side up on rack in open shallow roasting pan. The rack keeps the meat out of the drippings. (In some roasts, the ribs form a natural rack.) It is not necessary to baste.

Insert meat thermometer so tip is in center of thickest part of meat and does not touch bone or rest in fat. Do not add water. Do not cover.

Roast meat in 325° oven. (It is not necessary to preheat oven.) Roast to desired degree of doneness (see Timetable), using thermometer reading as final guide. Roasts are easier to carve if allowed to set 15 to 20 minutes after removing from oven. Since meat continues to cook after removal from oven, if roast is to "set," it should be removed from oven when thermometer registers 5° lower than the desired doneness.

You'll find some guidelines for carving a pork loin roast on page 124.

MUSTARD-TOMATO SAUCE

 2 egg yolks
½ cup sugar
½ cup undiluted condensed tomato soup
½ cup prepared mustard
½ cup butter or margarine
¼ cup vinegar

Mix all ingredients in saucepan. Cook over low heat, stirring constantly, until sauce thickens. This is one of our favorite accompaniments for pork roasts.

2 cups.

TIMETABLE

Cut	Approximate Weight	Meat Thermometer Reading	Approximate Cooking Time (Minutes per Pound)
Loin			
Center	3 to 5 pounds	170°	30 to 35
Half	5 to 7 pounds	170°	35 to 40
Blade or Sirloin	3 to 4 pounds	170°	40 to 45
Boneless Top (double)	3 to 5 pounds	170°	35 to 45
Boneless Top	2 to 4 pounds	170°	30 to 35
Picnic Shoulder			
Arm Picnic	5 to 8 pounds	170°	30 to 35
Rolled	3 to 5 pounds	170°	35 to 40
Blade Boston	4 to 6 pounds	170°	40 to 45
Leg (fresh ham)			
Whole (bone in)	12 to 14 pounds	170°	22 to 26
Boneless	10 to 14 pounds	170°	24 to 28
Half (bone in)	5 to 8 pounds	170°	35 to 40
Tenderloin	½ to 1 pound		¾ to 1 hour (total)
Spareribs, Back Ribs, Country-style Ribs*			1½ to 2½ hours (total)

*All three are always cooked until well done.

TO BROIL FRESH PORK

For each serving, allow about ½ to ¾ pound of chops and steaks with bone in, about ⅓ pound for boneless cuts.

Diagonally slash outer edge of fat on chops or steaks at 1-inch intervals to prevent curling (do not cut into lean). Set oven control at broil and/or 550°. Place meat on rack in broiler so top of meat is 3 to 5 inches from heat. Broil until light brown. The meat should be about half done (see Timetable).

If desired, season brown side with salt and pepper. (Always season after browning as salt tends to draw moisture to surface and delay browning.) Turn meat; broil until brown.

TIMETABLE

Cut	Approximate Cooking Time per Side
Chops (¾ to 1 inch)	10 to 12 minutes
Shoulder Steaks (½ to ¾ inch)	10 to 12 minutes
Patties (1 inch)	10 to 12 minutes
Kabobs (1½ × 1½ × ¾ inch)	11 to 12 minutes

PORK CHOP DINNER

  4 pork loin or rib chops, 1 inch thick
  ¼ cup water
  4 medium potatoes, pared
  4 small carrots
  4 medium onions
  1 teaspoon salt
  ¼ teaspoon pepper

Brown meat in large skillet over medium heat. Drain off fat. Add water and vegetables. Season with salt and pepper. Cover tightly; simmer 1 hour or until done.

Try this skillet meal with Pineapple-Marshmallow Slaw (page 53) and Herb-topped Rolls (page 68).

4 servings.

MEXICAN PORK CHOPS

  4 pork loin or rib chops, 1 inch thick
  1 teaspoon salt
  ⅛ teaspoon pepper
  1 medium green pepper, cut into 4 rings
  4 tablespoons uncooked instant rice
  1 can (about 16 ounces) stewed tomatoes

Brown meat over medium heat. Season with salt and pepper. Top each chop with a green pepper ring; fill each ring with 1 tablespoon rice. Carefully pour ¼ cup stewed tomatoes on rice in each ring. Pour remaining tomatoes into skillet. Cover tightly; simmer 1 hour or until done. Add a small amount of water if necessary.

Menu mates: lettuce wedges, Perky Lima Beans (page 59) and Graham Cracker Torte (page 78).

4 servings.

STUFFING-TOPPED PORK CHOPS

  6 pork loin or rib chops, 1 inch thick
  ½ cup water
  ¼ cup chopped celery
  2 tablespoons finely chopped onion
  2 tablespoons butter or margarine
  2 cups herb-seasoned stuffing
  1 can (8 ounces) cream-style corn

Heat oven to 350°. Arrange meat in ungreased baking dish, 13½ × 9 × 2 inches. Add the water and bake uncovered 45 minutes.

Cook and stir celery and onion in butter until tender; stir in stuffing and corn. Spoon ⅓ cup stuffing onto each chop. Bake uncovered 30 minutes longer.

Accompany with buttered spinach and Okra and Tomato Salad (page 54).

6 servings.

BRAISED PORK CHOPS

4 pork loin or rib chops, ½ to
  1 inch thick
1 teaspoon salt
¼ teaspoon pepper
¼ cup pineapple juice
  Pan Gravy (below)

Brown meat over medium heat. Season with salt and pepper. Reduce heat; pour pineapple juice on meat. Cover tightly; simmer ½-inch chops 20 to 25 minutes, 1-inch chops 30 to 35 minutes or until done. Serve with Pan Gravy.

Sprouts Sauté (page 60), an apple salad and mashed potatoes are nice serve-alongs for the braised chops. For dessert try Coconut Pudding (page 98).

4 servings.

PAN GRAVY

Place meat on warm platter; keep warm while making gravy. Pour drippings (fat and juices) into bowl, leaving brown particles in pan. Let fat rise to top of drippings; skim off fat, reserving ¼ cup. Place the ¼ cup reserved fat in pan. Blend in ¼ cup all-purpose flour. Cook over low heat, stirring until mixture is smooth and bubbly. Remove from heat. Stir in 2 cups water. Heat to boiling, stirring constantly. Boil and stir 1 minute. Season with salt and pepper.

2 cups.

Substitution

For pineapple juice: ¼ cup apple juice or ¼ cup water.

For Perfect Pan Gravy

Pan gravy is really very simple. Just follow the instructions carefully and rely on three little secrets to success:

☐ Be exact with the fat—too little makes the gravy lumpy.
☐ Be just as exact with the flour—too little makes the gravy greasy. And when you blend it into the fat, scrape the pan often as you go.
☐ Then boil for just a minute, stirring until smooth. You can even deepen the color with a few drops of bottled brown bouquet sauce.

BARBECUED RIBS

4½ pounds pork back ribs, cut into pieces
¼ cup soy sauce
1 tablespoon plus 2 teaspoons cornstarch
1 bottle (18 ounces) barbecue sauce

Arrange ribs meaty side up in open shallow roasting pan. Do not add water. Do not cover. Roast in 325° oven 1¾ hours.

Mix remaining ingredients; pour on meat. Bake uncovered about 45 minutes longer or until meat is done.

Team up with Best Tossed Salad (page 53) and Hopping John (page 74), a zesty combo of black-eye peas and rice.

5 or 6 servings.

Substitution

For back ribs: 4½ pounds spareribs.

BAKED SPARERIBS

Arrange 3 to 4 pounds spareribs meaty side up in open shallow roasting pan. Do not add water. Do not cover. Roast in 325° oven 1½ to 2½ hours or until meat is done.

4 servings.

GLAZED BARBECUED SPARERIBS

4 servings ready-to-eat barbecued spareribs
¼ cup orange marmalade, melted
2 tablespoons lemon juice

Heat oven to 300°. Arrange spareribs meaty side up in ungreased baking pan, 13×9×2 inches. Mix marmalade and lemon juice; spoon onto ribs. Heat uncovered 25 minutes or until heated through.

While you're at the deli, pick up some coleslaw and potato salad. Garnish them prettily and no one will guess you didn't do it *all* yourself.

4 servings.

Substitution

For orange marmalade: ¼ cup lime marmalade.

PINEAPPLE-STUFFED SPARERIBS

    1 rack spareribs (about 3 pounds)
    ¼ cup chopped celery
    2 tablespoons chopped onion
    2 tablespoons butter or margarine
    1 can (13¼ ounces) pineapple chunks,
         drained (reserve syrup)
    ½ teaspoon cloves
    2 cups packaged seasoned stuffing

Tie spareribs in circle; place bone tips up on rack in open shallow roasting pan. Do not add water. Do not cover. Roast in 325° oven 2 hours.

Cook and stir celery and onion in butter until tender. Mix with pineapple, cloves, stuffing and enough reserved pineapple syrup to moisten. Spoon dressing into circle of ribs; bake uncovered 30 minutes longer or until meat is done.

4 servings.

GLAZED RIBS

    4 pounds spareribs
    1 can (15 ounces) tomato sauce
    1 envelope (.7 ounce) onion salad
         dressing mix
    ¼ cup vinegar
    ¼ cup light molasses
    2 tablespoons salad oil
    1 teaspoon dry mustard
    1 cup water

Heat oven to 350°. Arrange spareribs meaty side up in open shallow roasting pan. Heat remaining ingredients to boiling, stirring constantly. Boil and stir 3 minutes. Pour sauce on meat. Bake uncovered about 1½ hours, basting 4 or 5 times.

Buttered Brussels sprouts and Oven Steamed Rice (page 73) are nice accompaniments.

4 servings.

Substitution

   For spareribs: 4 pounds pork back ribs or country-style ribs.

TENDERLOIN PATTIES SUPREME

    6 pork tenderloin patties, 1 inch thick
         Salt
    6 onion slices, ¼ inch thick
    ¼ cup catsup
    ⅓ cup lemon-lime carbonated beverage
    1 teaspoon Worcestershire sauce
    ⅛ teaspoon chili powder

Season patties with salt; arrange in ungreased baking pan, 9×9×2 inches. Top each patty with an onion slice. Bake patties uncovered in 325° oven 30 minutes.

Mix remaining ingredients; pour on patties. Bake uncovered 30 minutes longer. Serve patties with sauce.

Pork patties for a party? Sure! Dress them up with Green Beans and Bacon (page 58) and Poppy Seed Noodles (page 72). For dessert, Lemon Pudding Shells (page 98).

4 servings.

PORK AND FRUIT SKILLET

       Uncooked instant rice (enough for
         6 servings)
    1 can (13¼ ounces) pineapple chunks,
         drained (reserve syrup)
    1 package (about 17½ ounces) frozen
         breaded pork patties (10)
    1 cup bottled sweet and sour sauce
    ½ cup dried or canned apricot halves
    ½ cup water

Cook rice as directed on package except—substitute reserved pineapple syrup for part of the water. Cook pork patties as directed on package.

While meat cooks, heat pineapple chunks, sweet and sour sauce, apricot halves and water to boiling. Reduce heat; simmer uncovered 10 minutes. Spoon sauce on pork patties. Serve with rice.

For a quick-as-can-be meal, serve with buttered peas and Pudding-Pie Dessert (page 98).

5 or 6 servings.

Pictured at left:
Pineapple-stuffed Spareribs—a new twist to a
proven family favorite.

CHEESE-TOPPED PORK CUTLETS

Pound 1½ pounds pork cutlets to flatten. Season with salt and pepper. Dip in beaten egg, then coat with dry bread crumbs. Melt shortening in large skillet; brown meat over medium heat. Pour in small amount of water. Cover tightly; simmer 30 minutes.

Arrange cutlets in lightly oiled baking pan; sprinkle 1 package (4 ounces) shredded Cheddar cheese on meat. Set oven control at broil and/or 550°. Broil until cheese is bubbly.

6 servings.

CHINESE PORK AND RICE

- ⅔ cup uncooked regular rice
- 1 medium onion, chopped
- 2 stalks celery, cut into diagonal slices
- 2 tablespoons salad oil
- 1½ cups boiling water
- 1 teaspoon instant chicken or beef bouillon
- 2 tablespoons soy sauce
- 2 cups cut-up cooked pork (¾- to 1-inch pieces)
- 1 medium green pepper, chopped

In large skillet, cook and stir rice, onion and celery in oil over medium heat until rice is golden brown and onion is tender. Stir in remaining ingredients except green pepper and heat to boiling. Reduce heat.

Cover tightly; simmer 18 to 20 minutes or until rice is tender and liquid absorbed. Stir in green pepper. Cover tightly; simmer 10 minutes longer.

Serve with a salad of tossed greens sparked with watermelon pickles.

4 servings.

Note: Be sure to use regular rice—not converted or instant.

Substitution

For instant bouillon: 1 chicken or beef bouillon cube.

SUBGUM

- 1 can (4 ounces) sliced mushrooms
- 2 cups diced cooked pork
- 4 stalks celery, sliced (about 2 cups)
- 1 tablespoon butter or margarine
- 1½ cups gravy
- 1 can (20 ounces) bean sprouts, drained
  Chow mein noodles

Cook and stir mushrooms (with liquid), pork and celery in butter until celery is tender, about 10 minutes. Stir in gravy; reduce heat. Cover tightly; simmer 15 minutes. Stir in bean sprouts; heat through. Serve on chow mein noodles.

4 servings.

Substitution

For chow mein noodles: Hot cooked rice.

BAKED MEAT SANDWICH

- 1 pound ground lean pork
- ½ cup chopped onion
- ½ cup shredded Swiss cheese
- ¼ cup grated Parmesan cheese
- 1 egg, slightly beaten
- 2 tablespoons snipped parsley
- 1½ teaspoons salt
- ¼ teaspoon red pepper sauce
  Rolled Biscuit dough
- 2 tablespoons mayonnaise or salad dressing

Heat oven to 400°. Grease baking pan, 8 × 8 × 2 inches, or 4 individual casseroles. In large skillet, cook and stir pork and onion until pork is light brown. Drain off fat. Stir in cheeses, egg, parsley, salt and pepper sauce. Remove from heat.

Prepare Biscuit dough for 10 to 12 biscuits as directed on buttermilk baking mix package except— add mayonnaise with the water. With floured fingers, pat half the dough into pan. Spread meat mixture on dough. Turn remaining dough onto meat mixture; with floured fingers, pat on meat. Bake uncovered 25 to 30 minutes. Especially delicious with cheese or mushroom sauce.

4 to 6 servings.

Substitution

For pork: 1 pound ground beef.

BAKED HAM

Select ham or other cut from those listed in chart below. Allow about ½ pound per person—less for boneless roasts, more for a roast with a bone. Place ham fat side up on rack in open shallow roasting pan. The rack keeps the meat out of the drippings. It is not necessary to baste.

Insert meat thermometer so tip is in center of thickest part of meat and does not touch bone or rest in fat. Do not add water. Do not cover.

Roast meat in 325° oven. (It is not necessary to preheat oven.) Roast to desired degree of doneness (see Timetable), using thermometer reading as final guide.

Ham is easier to carve if allowed to set 15 to 20 minutes after removing from oven. Since meat continues to cook after removal from oven, if ham is to "set," it should be removed when thermometer registers 5° lower than desired doneness.

You'll find some guidelines for carving a whole ham on page 124.

GLAZED BAKED HAM

Pictured on page 5.

For a glazed ham, remove ham 30 minutes before it is done. Pour drippings from pan. Score fat surface of ham lightly, cutting uniform diamond shapes. A whole clove can be inserted in each. Pour on Orange Glaze (below); continue baking 30 minutes, basting as directed. Or use any of the commercial glazes now available in supermarkets, but be sure to follow the directions on the label.

ORANGE GLAZE

1 can (6 ounces) frozen orange
  juice concentrate (thawed)
¼ cup brown sugar (packed)
¼ teaspoon cloves
¼ teaspoon cinnamon

Mix all ingredients. Pour half the glaze on ham. Baste ham occasionally with remaining glaze during the last 30 minutes of baking time.

Enough for a 4-pound ham.

TIMETABLE

Cut	Approximate Weight	Meat Thermometer Reading	Approximate Cooking Time (Minutes per Pound)
Ham (cook before eating)			
Whole	10 to 14 pounds	160°	18 to 20
Half	5 to 7 pounds	160°	22 to 25
Shank Portion	3 to 4 pounds	160°	35 to 40
Rump Portion	3 to 4 pounds	160°	35 to 40
Ham (fully cooked)			
Whole	10 to 15 pounds	140°	15 to 18
Half	5 to 7 pounds	140°	18 to 24
Loin	3 to 5 pounds	160°	25 to 30
Arm Picnic (cook before eating)	5 to 8 pounds	170°	35
Arm Picnic (fully cooked)	5 to 8 pounds	140°	25 to 30
Shoulder Roll	2 to 3 pounds	170°	35 to 40
Canadian-style Bacon	2 to 4 pounds	160°	35 to 40
Ham Loaf	2 pounds	160°	1½ hours (total)
Ham Patties	1 inch thick		¾ to 1 hour (total)

SMOKED HAM SLICE

Allow about ½ to ¾ pound for each serving. Diagonally slash outer edge of fat at 1-inch intervals to prevent curling. Then proceed with your favorite method of cooking.

To Bake: Place 1-inch-thick ham slice in ungreased baking dish. If desired, spread with ¼ cup favorite jelly, slightly beaten, or Brown Sugar Glaze: Mix ½ cup brown sugar (packed), ¼ teaspoon dry mustard and 1½ teaspoons vinegar. Bake uncovered in 325° oven 30 minutes.

To Panfry: Rub skillet with small piece of fat cut from slice. Cook ½-inch-thick ham slice over medium heat about 3 minutes or until light brown. Turn ham slice; cook about 3 minutes longer.

To Broil: Set oven control at broil and/or 550°. Place 1-inch-thick ham slice on rack in broiler pan so top of ham slice is 3 inches from heat. Broil about 10 minutes or until light brown. Turn ham slice; broil about 6 minutes longer. If desired, after turning and during last 2 minutes of broiling, brush with 3 tablespoons jelly, slightly beaten.

HAM 'N LIMAS

   1 **package (10 ounces) frozen baby
      lima beans**
   1 **fully cooked smoked ham slice,
      1 inch thick**
   1 **cup shredded Cheddar cheese (4 ounces)**

Cook lima beans as directed on package; drain. Diagonally slash outer edge of fat on ham slice at 1-inch intervals to prevent curling.

Set oven control at broil and/or 550°. Broil ham 3 inches from heat about 10 minutes or until light brown. Turn meat; broil 6 minutes longer. Top with lima beans and sprinkle with cheese. Broil about 2 minutes or until cheese is melted and bubbly.

For family or for company, serve with Cinnamon-Applesauce Salad (page 56), Corn Sesame Sauté (page 61) and Perfect Pineapple Pie (page 84).

4 to 6 servings.

Substitution

   For frozen lima beans: 1 can (8 ounces) lima beans, drained.

TAHITIAN HAM DINNER

   1 **fully cooked smoked ham slice,
      ¾ inch thick (about 1½ pounds)**
   2 **packages (10 ounces each) frozen
      Brussels sprouts**
   2 **tablespoons water**
   1 **or 2 bananas
      Sauce (below)**

Place 30 × 18-inch piece of heavy-duty aluminum foil in jelly roll pan, 15½ × 10½ × 1 inch. Place ham slice on foil; arrange Brussels sprouts around ham. Sprinkle water on Brussels sprouts. Fold foil over meat and seal securely. Cook in 400° oven 40 minutes.

Open foil packet; fold edges back, keeping Brussels sprouts covered. Diagonally slice bananas onto meat. Pour Sauce on bananas.

Set oven control at broil and/or 550°. Broil 4 to 5 inches from heat 5 minutes or until Sauce is bubbly and brown.

6 or 7 servings.

SAUCE

Heat 12 large marshmallows (or 1 cup miniature marshmallows), 3 tablespoons milk and 2 tablespoons butter or margarine over medium heat, stirring constantly, just until marshmallows are melted.

SCALLOPED POTATOES "AND"

Prepare 1 package (5.5 ounces) scalloped potatoes as directed except—try one of the additions below:

■ *Canadian-style Bacon:* Before baking, top with four ½-inch-thick slices Canadian-style bacon. Bake 30 to 35 minutes.

■ *Ham Cubes:* Omit butter; stir in 1½ cups cubed cooked ham. Bake 35 to 40 minutes.

■ *Sausage:* Omit butter; top with 1 package (8 ounces) fully cooked brown and serve link sausage. Bake 35 to 40 minutes.

4 servings.

HAM CASSEROLE

  1 **cup shredded Cheddar cheese
     (4 ounces)**
  ½ **cup light cream or half-and-half**
  2 **cups diced cooked potatoes**
1½ **to 2 cups cubed cooked ham**
  2 **tablespoons chopped pimiento**

Heat oven to 350°. In medium saucepan, heat cheese and cream, stirring constantly, until cheese melts and sauce is creamy. Remove from heat. Stir in remaining ingredients. Pour into ungreased 1½-quart casserole. Cover tightly; bake 45 minutes.

Brussels and Carrots Salad (page 54) is a colorful salad that's perfect with this family favorite.

4 servings.

Substitution

For ham: 1½ to 2 cups cubed pork luncheon meat.

RAVIOLI-SAUSAGE CASSEROLE

1 **can (4 ounces) mushroom stems
   and pieces, drained**
1 **can (15½ ounces) ravioli in tomato sauce**
¼ **cup catsup**
1 **green pepper, finely chopped**
1 **cup shredded mozzarella cheese
   (4 ounces)**
1 **package (8 ounces) fully cooked brown and
   serve link sausage**

Heat oven to 350°. Mix mushrooms, ravioli in tomato sauce and catsup.

In ungreased 1-quart casserole, alternate layers of ⅓ of the ravioli mixture and ½ each green pepper and cheese. Arrange sausage spoke-fashion on top. Bake uncovered 45 minutes or until bubbly.

Best Tossed Salad (page 53) and hot French bread are the simple but perfect asides for this double-quick casserole.

6 to 8 servings.

LAYERED HAM DINNER

1 **package (9 ounces) frozen
   cut green beans**
1 **can (10¾ ounces) condensed
   cream of celery soup**
¼ **cup mayonnaise**
1 **tablespoon prepared mustard**
2 **packages (3 or 4 ounces each)
   thinly sliced cooked ham**
1 **cup shredded Cheddar cheese (4 ounces)**
¼ **cup dry bread crumbs**

Heat oven to 350°. Rinse beans with small amount of running cold water to separate and remove ice crystals; drain. Place beans in ungreased 1½-quart casserole.

Mix soup, mayonnaise and mustard; spoon half the mixture on beans. Top with ham and spoon remaining soup mixture on meat. Sprinkle with cheese and bread crumbs. Bake uncovered 20 minutes.

To accompany this hearty casserole, we suggest Orange-Cauliflower Salad (page 56) and parsley buttered potatoes.

4 to 6 servings.

Substitution

For packaged ham: ½ pound fully cooked ham, cut into julienne strips.

SAUSAGE AND KRAUT ROMANOFF

1 **package (5.5 ounces) noodles Romanoff**
1 **package (8 ounces) fully cooked
   brown and serve link sausage, sliced**
½ **teaspoon caraway seed**
1 **can (8 ounces) sauerkraut, drained**

Heat oven to 375°. Prepare noodles Romanoff as directed on package for oven method except—stir in sausage slices, caraway seed and sauerkraut before baking.

Bright Bean Salad (page 54) provides the just-right color and flavor accent.

4 servings.

Pineapple-Cherry Bologna

Chili Dogs

PINEAPPLE-CHERRY BOLOGNA

1-pound ring bologna
Pineapple-Cherry Glaze (below)
Instant mashed potatoes (enough for 4 servings)

If necessary, remove casing from bologna; arrange in ungreased 9-inch pie pan. Cut ring diagonally at 2-inch intervals, not cutting completely through. Separate cuts and spoon in part of glaze. Spread remaining glaze on top of bologna.

Heat oven to 400°. Prepare mashed potatoes as directed on package. Mound potatoes in center of ring. Bake 20 minutes or until potatoes are light brown.

4 servings.

PINEAPPLE-CHERRY GLAZE

½ **cup crushed pineapple**
¼ **cup coarsely chopped maraschino cherries**
¼ **cup light corn syrup**
2 **tablespoons white vinegar**
¼ **teaspoon cloves**
2 **drops red food color**
1½ **teaspoons water**
1½ **teaspoons cornstarch**

Heat pineapple, cherries, corn syrup, vinegar, cloves and food color to boiling, stirring occasionally. Reduce heat; simmer 15 minutes. Blend water and cornstarch; stir into fruit. Cook, stirring constantly, until mixture thickens and boils. Boil and stir 1 minute.

POLISH SAUSAGE BOIL

Pictured on page 5.

1 **pound fully cooked Polish sausage**
½ **to ¾ cup beer**

In covered skillet, simmer Polish sausage in beer 10 minutes. (If using uncooked Polish sausage, increase cooking time to 20 minutes.)

Sauerkraut or Scalloped Potato Salad (page 67) and dark pumpernickel buns are perfect go-withs.

4 servings.

Substitution

For beer: ½ to ¾ cup water.

PEASANT'S FEAST

- 1 **can (16 ounces) sauerkraut**
- 1 **can (16 ounces) tomatoes**
- 1 **medium onion, thinly sliced**
- 2 **tablespoons brown sugar, if desired**
- ½ **teaspoon salt**
- 4 **medium baking potatoes**
- 1 **package (12 ounces) smoked small sausage links**
  Butter
  Snipped parsley

Heat oven to 350°. Mix sauerkraut, tomatoes, onion, sugar and salt in ungreased baking dish, 11½ × 7½ × 1½ inches. Rub potatoes with shortening and prick with fork; arrange on sauerkraut mixture. Bake uncovered 1 hour.

Add sausages, covering each with sauerkraut mixture. Bake uncovered 30 minutes longer or until potatoes are done. Make crosswise slits on potatoes; squeeze until some potato pops up through opening. Slip butter into opening and sprinkle with parsley.

All this meal-in-one needs is a simple green salad.

4 servings.

Substitution

For sausage links: About 1 pound Polish sausage or 2-pound piece large bologna (if necessary, remove casing; score top of piece and place on sauerkraut mixture).

FRANKFURTER CASSEROLE

- 6 **frankfurters, cut into 1-inch pieces**
- 1 **package (9 ounces) frozen cut green beans, broken apart**
- 1 **can (11 ounces) condensed Cheddar cheese soup**
- 1 **cup unseasoned croutons**

Heat oven to 375°. Mix frankfurters, green beans and soup. Pour into greased 1½-quart casserole. Sprinkle with croutons. Bake uncovered 30 minutes or until sauce is bubbly.

6 servings.

Substitution

For cheese soup: 1 cup cheese sauce.

CREOLE WIENERS

- 8 **slices bacon, diced**
- 3 **cups minced onion**
- 1 **can (16 ounces) tomatoes**
- ¾ **teaspoon salt**
- ⅛ **teaspoon pepper**
- 1 **pound frankfurters**

Fry bacon and onion in large skillet until bacon is crisp and onion is tender. Drain off all but 2 tablespoons fat. Stir in tomatoes, salt and pepper.

Heat to boiling. Reduce heat; simmer 15 minutes, stirring occasionally. Stir in frankfurters. Cover tightly; simmer 15 minutes.

Menu plan: Oven Steamed Rice (page 73), green beans and Chocolate-Cherry Parfait (page 98).

5 or 6 servings.

CHILI DOGS

- 12 **frankfurters**
- 1 **slice American cheese, 3½ × 3½ inches**
- 2 **cans (15 ounces each) chili hot beans**
- 1 **can (8 ounces) tomato sauce**
- ¼ **teaspoon chili powder**
- ¼ **teaspoon cumin**
- ⅛ **teaspoon cayenne red pepper, if desired**

Heat oven to 400°. Make three ½-inch-deep diagonal cuts at regular intervals in each frankfurter. Cut cheese slice into 36 strips, about 1 × ¼ inch. Insert cheese strip in each frankfurter cut.

Mix beans, tomato sauce and seasonings in ungreased baking dish, 11½ × 7½ × 1½ inches. Arrange franks on beans. Bake 20 to 25 minutes.

Superstar supper plan for a teenage bash: fresh vegetable relishes and Bun Sticks (page 68) for the crunch; Chocolate Fondue (page 94) for smooth and sweet swirling.

4 or 5 servings.

Substitutions

For frankfurters: 1 package (12 ounces) smoked small sausage links.

For chili hot beans: 2 cans (15½ ounces each) kidney beans.

For seasonings: 1 envelope (1¼ ounces) chili seasoning mix.

Lamb

TO ROAST LAMB

Select roast, allowing about ½ to ¾ pound per person. Do not remove "fell" (the paperlike covering). Roasts keep their shape better, cook in less time and are juicier when the "fell" is left on. If desired, season meat with salt and pepper.

Place meat fat side up on rack in open shallow roasting pan. It is not necessary to baste; the meat does its own basting.

Insert meat thermometer so tip is in center of thickest part of meat and does not touch bone or rest in fat. Do not add water. Do not cover.

Roast meat in 325° oven. Roast to desired degree of doneness (see Timetable), using thermometer reading as final guide. Lamb is done when meat thermometer registers 175 to 180°.

Roasts are easier to carve if allowed to set 15 minutes. If roast is to "set," it should be removed from oven when thermometer registers 5 to 10° lower than the desired doneness.

See page 124 for carving tips.

TIMETABLE

Cut	Approximate Weight	Approximate Cooking Time (Minutes per Pound)
Shoulder		
Square	4 to 6 pounds	30 to 35
Boneless	3 to 5 pounds	40 to 45
Cushion	3 to 5 pounds	30 to 35
Crown Roast	4 to 6 pounds	40 to 45
Rib*	1½ to 3 pounds	35 to 45
Leg	5 to 8 pounds	30 to 35
Rolled Leg	3 to 5 pounds	35 to 40

*Roast at 375°

TO BROIL LAMB CHOPS

Remove "fell" (the paperlike covering) if it is on chops. Diagonally slash outer edge of fat on meat at 1-inch intervals to prevent curling. Set oven control at broil and/or 550°. Place chops on rack in broiler pan so tops of ¾- to 1-inch chops are 2 to 3 inches from heat, 1- to 2-inch chops are 3 to 5 inches from heat. Broil until brown. The chops should be about half done (see Timetable).

If desired, season *brown* side with salt and pepper. Turn chops; broil until brown.

TIMETABLE

Thickness	Approximate Cooking Time per Side*
1 inch	6 to 7 minutes
1½ inches	9 to 10 minutes
2 inches	10 to 11 minutes

*Time given is for medium doneness; lamb chops are not usually served rare.

PRINCESS LAMB CHOPS

    4 lamb shoulder chops, 1 inch thick
    ½ cup red wine
    ½ cup salad oil
    1 tablespoon vinegar
    2 tablespoons chopped green onion
    1 teaspoon grated lemon peel
 1½ teaspoons salt
    ½ teaspoon pepper
    ¼ teaspoon dry mustard
    ⅛ teaspoon thyme
    ⅛ teaspoon basil
    ⅛ teaspoon instant minced garlic

Place meat in shallow glass dish. Mix remaining ingredients; pour on meat. Cover; refrigerate at least 2 hours, turning meat occasionally.

Set oven control at broil and/or 550°. Place meat on rack in broiler pan. Brush some of the marinade on meat. Broil 3 inches from heat 7 minutes. Brush meat with marinade; turn and brush again. Broil 5 minutes longer.

4 servings.

Substitutions

For wine: ½ cup apple juice.
For instant garlic: 1 clove garlic, minced.

MIXED GRILL

Pictured on page 5.

- **6 lamb kidneys**
- **6 lamb loin or rib chops, 1 inch thick**
- **6 pork sausage links**
- **1 teaspoon salt**
- **6 tomato slices, ½ inch thick**
- **½ teaspoon salt**
- **¼ teaspoon pepper**
- **¼ teaspoon basil leaves**
- **6 large fresh mushroom caps, washed and trimmed**
- **1 tablespoon butter or margarine, melted**

Wash kidneys; split each in half. Remove membrane, hard parts and white veins. Arrange kidneys, lamb chops and sausages on rack in broiler pan. Set oven control at broil and/or 550°. Broil 3 inches from heat 7 minutes. Season chops and kidneys with 1 teaspoon salt; turn meats.

Place tomato slices on rack. Mix ½ teaspoon salt, the pepper and basil leaves; sprinkle on tomatoes. Place mushroom caps rounded side up on rack; brush with butter.

Broil 5 minutes, brushing mushrooms with butter once during broiling. Season chops and kidneys with salt. To serve, arrange a chop, kidney, sausage link, mushroom cap and tomato slice on each plate.

Carrots Bouillon (page 60) and Best Tossed Salad (page 53) add just the right color accents.

6 servings.

Substitutions

For kidneys: 6 chicken livers or 6 small pieces of calf liver.

For sausage: 6 slices bacon.

Charcoal-grilled Lamb Chops

Beautifully juicy and slightly pink—that's how charcoal-grilled lamb chops should be. And are, with a little know-how. Choose loin, rib or shoulder chops, one or two to a person. Trim off the excess fat and place the chops on grill 4 inches from medium coals. Grill ¾-inch chops 10 to 12 minutes on each side; for 1-inch chops, make it 14 to 16 minutes. Test for doneness by making a knife slit along the bone. Perfect!

LAMB OSSOBUCO

- **¼ cup all-purpose flour**
- **1 teaspoon salt**
- **¼ teaspoon pepper**
- **4 lamb shanks (about ¾ pound each)**
- **⅓ cup shortening**
- **½ cup tomato sauce**
- **½ cup white wine**
- **½ cup water**
- **½ teaspoon instant beef bouillon**
- **2 carrots, chopped**
- **3 stalks celery, chopped**
- **⅛ teaspoon each oregano, thyme, rosemary and basil**

Mix flour, salt and pepper; coat meat with flour mixture. Melt shortening in large skillet or Dutch oven; brown meat over medium heat, turning occasionally. Drain off fat.

Reduce heat; stir in remaining ingredients. Cover tightly; simmer 2 hours or until meat is tender. If you like, thicken broth.

Nice with lettuce wedges, Skillet Pilaf (page 73) and French bread.

4 to 6 servings.

CURRIED LAMB AND BARLEY CASSEROLE

- **1 pound boneless lamb, cut into 1-inch cubes**
- **¾ cup uncooked barley**
- **2 cups water**
- **1 can (16 ounces) whole tomatoes**
- **1 tablespoon plus 1 teaspoon instant chopped onion**
- **1 tablespoon parsley flakes**
- **2 teaspoons salt**
- **½ teaspoon curry powder**

Heat oven to 350°. Mix all ingredients in ungreased 2½-quart casserole. Cover tightly; bake 2 hours or until barley is tender and liquid is absorbed.

Perfect with Brussels and Carrots Salad (page 54).

4 servings.

Substitutions

For instant onion: 4 tablespoons chopped onion.
For parsley flakes: 1 tablespoon snipped parsley.

Veal

TO ROAST VEAL

Select roast, allowing about ½ pound per person—less for boneless roasts, more for roasts with a bone. If desired, season with salt and pepper before, during or after roasting.

Place meat fat side up on rack in open shallow roasting pan. The rack keeps the meat out of the drippings. (In roasts such as rib roasts or racks, the ribs form a natural rack.) If roast has little or no fat, place 2 or 3 slices bacon or salt pork on top.

Insert meat thermometer so tip is in center of thickest part of meat and does not touch bone or rest in fat. Do not add water. Do not cover.

Roast meat in 325° oven. (It is not necessary to preheat oven.) Roast to desired degree of doneness (see Timetable), using thermometer reading as final guide. Veal is done when meat thermometer registers 170°.

Roasts are easier to carve if allowed to set 15 to 20 minutes after removing from oven. If roast is to "set," remove from oven when thermometer registers 5 to 10° lower than the desired doneness.

TIMETABLE

Cut	Approximate Weight	Approximate Cooking Time (Minutes per Pound)
Round or Sirloin	5 to 8 pounds	25 to 35
Loin	4 to 6 pounds	30 to 35
Rib	3 to 5 pounds	35 to 40
Boneless Rump	3 to 5 pounds	40 to 45
Boneless Shoulder	4 to 6 pounds	40 to 45

SAVORY VEAL ROAST

4-pound veal boneless rump or sirloin roast
1 teaspoon salt
¼ teaspoon pepper
¼ cup soy sauce
¼ teaspoon garlic powder

Place meat fat side up on rack in open shallow roasting pan. Season with salt and pepper. If roast has little or no fat, place 2 or 3 slices bacon on top. Insert meat thermometer so tip is in center of thickest part of meat. Do not add water. Do not cover.

Roast in 325° oven 2½ to 3 hours or until thermometer registers 170°. During last hour of baking, baste often with mixture of soy sauce and garlic powder.

Wondering what to serve with the roast? We like Cheese Potato Casserole (page 65) and Snow Peas and Carrot Nuggets (page 62).

6 to 8 servings.

VEAL PAPRIKA

⅓ cup all-purpose flour
3 teaspoons salt
2 teaspoons paprika
⅛ teaspoon pepper
2 pounds boneless veal, cut into 1-inch cubes
3 tablespoons shortening
⅛ teaspoon instant minced garlic
2 cups dairy sour cream
   Poppy Seed Noodles (page 72)

Heat oven to 350°. Mix flour, salt, paprika and pepper; coat meat with flour mixture. Melt shortening in large skillet. Add garlic and meat; brown meat thoroughly. Remove from heat; stir in sour cream. Cover tightly; bake 1 hour. Serve on Poppy Seed Noodles.

Marinated Cucumber Salad (page 54) adds just the right degree of contrast—in flavor and texture.

6 servings.

Substitution

For instant garlic: 1 clove garlic, minced.

VEAL WITH TOMATO SAUCE

6 veal cutlets (about 4 ounces each)
¼ cup salad oil
2 cloves garlic, crushed
1 cup thinly sliced onion
1 jar (3 ounces) sliced mushrooms, drained
2 tablespoons flour
1 teaspoon salt
¼ teaspoon pepper
1 can (8 ounces) tomato sauce
⅔ cup water

Pound meat until ¼ inch thick. In large skillet, heat oil and garlic over medium-high heat. Brown meat quickly, about 5 minutes. Remove meat from skillet.

Reduce heat to medium. Add onion and mushrooms; cook and stir until onion is tender. Stir in flour, salt and pepper; pour in tomato sauce and water. Heat to boiling, stirring constantly. Boil and stir 1 minute. Return meat to skillet. Cover tightly; simmer about 30 minutes or until tender.

Theme your whole menu Italian with Green and White Salad (page 53), buttered spaghetti and Parmesan Supper Bread (page 71). Fruit Dessert Freeze (page 95) is a refreshing finish.

6 servings.

Substitution

For canned mushrooms: 2 cups sliced fresh mushrooms (¼ pound).

Coping with Cutlets

Most veal cutlet recipes call for meat that's ¼ inch thick. Sometimes you can buy the cutlets that way; sometimes you have to do the pounding yourself. You can even buy veal round steak and do both the cutting *and* the pounding. It's up to you—and your budget.

If you're a do-it-yourselfer, start with ½-inch-thick cutlets or steaks. To pound down to ¼ inch, use a metal or wooden mallet—or even the dull edge of a knife or cleaver. Or do as grandma did and use the edge of a saucer. However you get them pounded, do make sure they're ¼ inch thick so you'll have no problem with the cooking time in the recipes.

BREADED VEAL CUTLETS

Pictured on page 5.

½ cup all-purpose flour*
1 teaspoon salt
½ teaspoon paprika
¼ teaspoon pepper
4 veal cutlets (about 4 ounces each)
1 egg
2 tablespoons water
1 cup dry bread crumbs
¼ cup shortening
1 lemon, cut into wedges

Mix flour, salt, paprika and pepper; coat meat with flour mixture. Pound until ¼ inch thick. Beat egg and water slightly. Dip meat into egg, then coat with bread crumbs.

Melt shortening in large skillet; brown meat quickly. Reduce heat. Cover tightly; cook about 45 minutes or until done. Serve with lemon wedges.

4 servings.

If using self-rising flour, decrease salt to ½ teaspoon.

VEAL MUSTARD

4 veal rib or loin chops, ¾ inch thick
1 teaspoon salt
½ teaspoon pepper
3 tablespoons prepared mustard
½ cup diced bacon
¾ cup light cream (20%) or half-and-half
2 tablespoons drained capers

Heat oven to 350°. Season meat with salt and pepper; spread mustard on both sides. Arrange meat in ungreased baking pan, 9×9×2 inches. Sprinkle bacon on and around meat. Bake uncovered 1 hour 15 minutes. Place meat on warm platter; keep warm while making sauce.

Drain off all but 1 tablespoon fat, leaving bacon and mustard in pan. Stir in cream and capers. Heat to boiling, stirring constantly. Reduce heat; simmer about 10 minutes or until sauce is consistency of thin white sauce. Pour sauce on chops.

4 servings.

Substitution

For veal rib or loin chops: 2 veal sirloin chops, cut in half.

Chicken

ROAST CHICKEN

Young chickens of any weight can be roasted, stuffed or unstuffed. A plump chicken, at least 2½ pounds, is particularly desirable. Allow about ¾ pound per serving. If desired, season cavity of chicken lightly with salt. Do not salt cavity if bird is to be stuffed.

Stuff chicken just before roasting—not ahead of time. (See Sausage Stuffing, right). Fill wishbone area with stuffing first. Fasten neck skin to back with skewer. Fold wings across back with tips touching. Fill body cavity lightly. (Do not pack—stuffing will expand while cooking.) Tie drumsticks to tail.

Heat oven (see Timetable). Brush chicken with melted butter or margarine. Place breast side up on rack in open shallow roasting pan. Do not add water. Do not cover.

Follow Timetable for approximate total cooking time. Chicken is done when drumstick meat feels very soft when pressed between fingers.

You'll find some guidelines for carving a roast chicken on page 124.

TIMETABLE

Ready-to-Cook Weight	Oven Temperature	Approximate Total Cooking Time
Broiler-fryer		
1½ to 2 pounds	400°	¾ to 1 hour
2 to 2½ pounds	400°	1 to 1¼ hours
2½ to 3 pounds	375°	1¼ to 1¾ hours
3 to 4 pounds	375°	1¾ to 2¼ hours
Capon (stuffed)		
5 to 8 pounds	325°	2½ to 3½ hours

GIBLETS

Wash gizzard, heart, liver and neck. Cover all except liver with water; season with ½ teaspoon salt, 2 peppercorns, 2 cloves, a small bay leaf and a little onion. Heat to boiling. Reduce heat; cover and simmer 1 to 2 hours or until gizzard is tender. Liver is very tender and can be fried, broiled or simmered in water, 5 to 10 minutes.

Giblet broth can be used in stuffing, gravy and recipes where chicken broth is specified. Cooked giblets can be cut up and added to gravy or stuffing. Refrigerate giblets and broth separately.

SAUSAGE STUFFING

Prepare 1 package (7 ounces) dry herbed stuffing mix as directed on package except—add ½ pound bulk pork sausage, crumbled and browned.

About 5 cups (enough for 5- to 8-pound chicken).

VARIATIONS

■ *Apple-Raisin Stuffing:* Omit sausage; add 1 medium apple, finely chopped, and ⅓ cup raisins.

■ *Pecan Stuffing:* Omit sausage; add 1 cup coarsely chopped pecans.

CHICKEN IN A POT

Pictured on page 36.

    1 apple, quartered
2½- to 3-pound broiler-fryer chicken
    2 tablespoons lemon juice
    2 teaspoons onion salt
    ½ teaspoon rosemary
    ⅛ teaspoon instant minced garlic

Heat oven to 375°. Place apple in cavity of chicken. Fold wings across back with tips touching. Place chicken breast side up in small Dutch oven or clay pot. (If using clay pot, line with parchment.) Brush chicken with lemon juice; season with remaining ingredients. Cover and bake about 1½ hours or until done.

4 servings.

Substitution

For instant garlic: 1 clove garlic, minced.

BROILED CHICKEN

Pictured on page 36.

Young chickens, weighing 2½ pounds or less, can be broiled. They should be halved, quartered or cut into pieces. If using chicken halves or quarters, turn wing tips onto back side.

Set oven control at broil and/or 550°. Brush chicken with melted butter or margarine. Place skin side down on rack in broiler pan; place broiler pan so top of chicken is 7 to 9 inches from heat. (If it is not possible to place the broiler pan this far from heat, reduce temperature to 450°.)

Broil chicken 30 minutes. Season brown side with salt and pepper. Turn chicken; if desired, brush again with butter or margarine. Broil 20 to 30 minutes longer or until brown, crisp and done.

FRIED CHICKEN

½ cup all-purpose flour*
1 teaspoon salt
½ teaspoon paprika
¼ teaspoon pepper
  Salad oil
2- to 3-pound broiler-fryer chicken, cut up

Mix flour, salt, paprika and pepper. Heat salad oil (¼ inch) in large skillet. Coat chicken with flour mixture. Brown chicken lightly in oil over medium heat, 15 to 20 minutes.

Reduce heat. Cover tightly; simmer 30 to 40 minutes or until done. (If skillet cannot be covered tightly, add 1 to 2 tablespoons water.) Turn chicken once or twice to assure even browning. Uncover for the last 5 minutes of cooking to crisp chicken.

Team this traditional favorite with something unexpected—perhaps Okra and Tomato Salad (page 54) and Curried Rice (page 74).

4 servings.

*If using self-rising flour, decrease salt to ½ teaspoon.

VARIATION

■ *Maryland Fried Chicken:* Beat 2 eggs and 2 tablespoons water. After coating chicken with flour, dip into egg, then coat with 2 cups cracker crumbs or dry bread crumbs.

OVEN-FRIED CHICKEN

¼ cup shortening
¼ cup butter or margarine
½ cup all-purpose flour*
1 teaspoon salt
1 teaspoon paprika
¼ teaspoon pepper
2½- to 3-pound broiler-fryer chicken, cut up

Heat oven to 425°. In oven, melt shortening and butter in baking pan, 13 × 9 × 2 inches. Mix flour, salt, paprika and pepper; coat chicken with flour mixture.

Arrange chicken skin side down in shortening. Bake uncovered 30 minutes. Turn chicken; bake uncovered 30 minutes longer or until done.

For a delicious dinner, accompany with baked potatoes, Peas and Almonds (page 62) and Raspberry Pie (page 83).

4 servings.

*If using self-rising flour, omit salt.

VARIATIONS

■ *Crusty-Curried Chicken:* Omit flour mixture; coat chicken with mixture of 1 cup buttermilk baking mix, 2 tablespoons curry powder, 1½ teaspoons salt and ¼ teaspoon pepper.

■ *Garlic Chip Chicken:* Omit flour mixture for coating chicken. In large skillet, melt ¼ cup butter or margarine with 1 teaspoon garlic salt, 1 teaspoon salt and ⅛ teaspoon pepper. Remove from heat. Finely crush 1 bag (5½ ounces) potato chips. Dip chicken into garlic butter, then coat with crushed chips.

GOLDEN PARMESAN CHICKEN

Pictured on page 5.

1¼ cups grated Parmesan cheese
 1 teaspoon salt
¼ teaspoon pepper
 3-pound broiler-fryer chicken, cut up
⅓ cup butter or margarine, melted

Heat oven to 425°. Grease baking pan, 13 × 9 × 2 inches. Mix cheese, salt and pepper. Dip chicken into butter, then coat with cheese mixture.

Arrange chicken skin side down in pan. Pour remaining butter on chicken. Bake uncovered 30 minutes. Turn chicken; bake uncovered 20 minutes longer or until done.

Blender Coleslaw (page 53) and potato salad play up to the Parmesan.

4 servings.

Note: This is delicious served cold. After baking, cool, cover and refrigerate.

BARBECUED CHICKEN

¼ cup butter or margarine
2½- to 3-pound broiler-fryer chicken, cut up
½ cup barbecue sauce
¼ cup frozen lemonade concentrate (thawed)
¼ cup water
 2 tablespoons instant minced onion

Heat oven to 425°. In oven, melt butter in baking pan, 13 × 9 × 2 inches. Place chicken in butter, turning to coat. Arrange skin side down in pan. Bake uncovered 30 minutes. Drain off fat; turn chicken.

Mix remaining ingredients; pour on chicken. Bake uncovered 30 minutes longer or until done, basting occasionally with sauce.

4 servings.

Substitution

For instant onion: ⅓ cup minced onion.

Pictured at left:
Broiled Chicken, Islander Chicken, Chicken in a Pot

ISLANDER CHICKEN

Pictured at left.

4 servings ready-to-eat fried chicken (about 12 pieces)
1 cup bottled sweet and sour sauce
8 large twist pretzels, if desired

Heat oven to 300°. Brush chicken with sauce. Arrange in ungreased baking pan, 13 × 9 × 2 inches. Bake uncovered 30 minutes or until heated through. Heat pretzels during the last 5 minutes.

With Snow Peas and Carrot Nuggets (page 62) and Mashed Potatoes flecked with green pepper (page 65), who would guess this meal started at the deli?

4 servings.

BARBECUED CHICKEN FIX-UP

 1 ready-to-eat barbecued chicken, split in half
¼ cup honey
¼ cup lemon juice
¼ teaspoon tarragon

Heat oven to 300°. Place chicken skin side up in ungreased baking pan, 13 × 9 × 2 inches. Mix remaining ingredients; pour on chicken. Bake uncovered about 25 minutes or until heated through.

Pick up a three-bean salad at the deli.

2 servings.

CHICKEN BAKE

2½-pound broiler-fryer chicken, cut up
 1 can (10¾ ounces) condensed cream of mushroom soup
½ envelope (about 1½-ounce size) onion soup mix

Heat oven to 375°. Arrange chicken skin side up in ungreased baking pan, 13 × 9 × 2 inches. Mix mushroom soup and onion soup mix (dry); pour on chicken. Cover tightly; bake 30 minutes. Uncover; bake 45 minutes longer or until done.

Need some menu help? We suggest Celery Seed Mashed Potatoes (page 65), Peas and Almonds (page 62), and Chocolate Chip Bars (page 90) with ice cream.

4 to 6 servings.

STEWED CHICKEN

3- to 4-pound broiler-fryer chicken, cut up
1 sprig parsley
1 celery stalk with leaves, cut up
1 carrot, sliced
1 small onion, sliced
2 teaspoons salt
½ teaspoon pepper

Place chicken with giblets and neck in kettle or Dutch oven. Add water to cover chicken. Add remaining ingredients; heat to boiling. Reduce heat. Cover tightly; simmer about 45 minutes or until done. Allow chicken to cool slightly in broth; refrigerate just until cool.

When cool, remove meat from bones and skin in pieces as large as possible. Skim fat from broth. Refrigerate broth and chicken pieces separately in covered containers; use within several days. For longer storage, package chicken and broth together and freeze.

3 to 4 cups cubed cooked chicken and 2 to 3½ cups broth.

Note: To cook a stewing chicken, select 4- to 5-pound stewing chicken. Simmer 2½ to 3½ hours or until tender.

About 5 cups cubed cooked chicken and 5 to 6 cups broth.

Concocting a Casserole?

Improvising, stretching or changing just for the sake of change? Whatever your reason for wanting to ad lib a bit, you can do so if you know how to figure.

To Equal:	Use:
2 cups cooked chicken or turkey	half of a 3- to 4-pound broiler-fryer or stewing chicken or 1½ to 2 pounds turkey pieces
1 cup cleaned cooked shrimp	¾ pound raw shrimp in the shell or 1 package (7 ounces) frozen peeled shrimp or 1 can (4½ to 5 ounces) shrimp
1 cup cooked rice	⅓ cup regular rice or ¼ cup converted rice or ½ cup instant (precooked) rice
2 cups cooked macaroni, spaghetti or noodles	3½ ounces macaroni or spaghetti or 4 ounces noodles

CAN-OPENER COMBO

1 can (16 ounces) French-style
   green beans, drained
1 can (10¾ ounces) condensed cream
   of mushroom soup
2 jars (5½ ounces each) boned chicken
½ teaspoon sage
   Chow mein noodles

Heat green beans, soup, chicken and sage, stirring occasionally. Serve on noodles.

A simple salad of lettuce wedges and your favorite dressing is just enough.

4 servings.

Substitution

For chicken: 1½ cups cooked cubed chicken or turkey.

CHICKEN AND MACARONI CASSEROLE

1½ cups uncooked elbow macaroni
      (about 5 ounces)
  1 cup shredded Cheddar cheese
      (4 ounces)
1½ cups cut-up cooked chicken
  1 can (4 ounces) mushroom stems and
      pieces, drained
 ¼ cup chopped pimiento
  1 can (10¾ ounces) condensed cream
      of chicken soup
  1 cup milk
 ½ teaspoon salt
 ½ teaspoon curry powder

Heat oven to 350°. Mix all ingredients in ungreased 1½-quart casserole. Cover tightly; bake 1 hour.

Complete the menu with broccoli, Cucumber Relish Mold (page 55) and Date or Mocha Brownies (page 88).

4 to 6 servings.

VARIATIONS

■ *Ham or Turkey and Macaroni Casserole:* Substitute 1½ cups cubed cooked ham or 1½ cups cubed cooked turkey for the chicken.

Turkey

ROAST TURKEY

Allow ¾ to 1 pound per serving when roasting turkeys under 12 pounds. For heavier birds, 12 pounds and over, allow ½ to ¾ pound per serving. If desired, season cavity of turkey lightly with salt. Do not salt cavity if turkey is to be stuffed.

Stuff turkey just before roasting. Fill wishbone area with stuffing first. Fasten neck skin to back with skewer. Fold wings across back with tips touching. Fill body cavity lightly. (Stuffing will expand.) Tuck drumsticks under band of skin or tie together with heavy string, then tie to tail.

Heat oven to 325°. Place turkey breast side up on rack in open shallow roasting pan. Brush with shortening, oil or butter. Insert meat thermometer so tip is in thickest part of inside thigh muscle or thickest part of breast meat and does not touch bone. Do not add water. Do not cover.

Follow Timetable. Place a tent of aluminum foil loosely over turkey when it starts to turn golden. When ⅔ done, cut band or string holding legs.

There is no substitute for a meat thermometer. It should register 185°. If the bird is stuffed, the point of the thermometer can be placed in the center of the stuffing and will register 165°. If a thermometer is not used, test for doneness about 30 minutes before Timetable so indicates. Move drumstick up and down—if done, the joint should give readily.

When turkey is done, remove from oven and allow to stand about 20 minutes for easiest carving. As soon as possible after serving, remove every bit of stuffing from turkey. Cool stuffing, meat and any gravy promptly; refrigerate separately. Use gravy or stuffing within 1 or 2 days; heat them thoroughly before serving. Serve cooked turkey meat within 2 or 3 days after roasting. If frozen, it can be kept up to 1 month.

See page 124 for carving tips.

TIMETABLE

Ready-to-Cook Weight	Approximate Total Cooking Time	Internal Temperature
6 to 8 pounds	3 to 3½ hours	185°
8 to 12 pounds	3½ to 4½ hours	185°
12 to 16 pounds	4½ to 5½ hours	185°
16 to 20 pounds	5½ to 6½ hours	185°
20 to 24 pounds	6½ to 7 hours	185°

This timetable is based on chilled or completely thawed turkeys at a temperature of about 40° and placed in preheated ovens. Times will be slightly less for unstuffed turkeys. Differences in the shape and tenderness of individual turkeys can also necessitate increasing or decreasing the cooking time slightly. For best results, use a meat thermometer. For prestuffed turkeys, follow package directions carefully; do not use timetable.

COOKING TURKEY IN FOIL

Prepare turkey as directed for Roast Turkey (at left). To wrap, place turkey breast side up in middle of large sheet of heavy-duty aluminum foil. (For larger birds, join two widths of foil.)

Brush with shortening, oil or butter. Place small pieces of aluminum foil over the ends of legs, tail and wing tips to prevent puncturing. Bring long ends of aluminum foil up over the breast of turkey and overlap 3 inches. Close open ends by folding up foil so drippings will not run into pan. Wrap loosely and do not seal airtight.

Heat oven to 450°. Place wrapped turkey, breast up, in open shallow roasting pan. Follow Timetable for approximate cooking time. Open foil once or twice during cooking to judge doneness. When thigh joint and breast meat begin to soften, fold back foil completely to brown turkey and crisp skin. Insert meat thermometer at this time.

TIMETABLE

Ready-to-Cook Weight	Approximate Total Cooking Time	Internal Temperature
7 to 9 pounds	2¼ to 2½ hours	185°
10 to 13 pounds	2¾ to 3 hours	185°
14 to 17 pounds	3½ to 4 hours	185°
18 to 21 pounds	4½ to 5 hours	185°
22 to 24 pounds	5½ to 6 hours	185°

HERBED TURKEY ROAST

3½- to 4-pound turkey roast
 1 cup white wine
 2 tablespoons butter or margarine, melted
 ½ teaspoon salt
 ⅛ teaspoon pepper
 ⅛ teaspoon sage
 ⅛ teaspoon thyme
 ¼ cup water
 2 tablespoons flour

Bake turkey roast as directed on package except—before roasting, mix wine, butter, salt, pepper, sage and thyme and pour on roast.

Remove roast from pan; keep warm. Skim fat from broth. Measure broth; return 1 cup to roasting pan. In tightly covered jar, shake water and flour; stir slowly into broth in pan. Heat to boiling, stirring constantly. Boil and stir 1 minute. Serve gravy with turkey.

Serve this elegant roast with elegant accompaniments: Honey-Chili Squash (page 63), Creamed Onions and Broccoli (page 62), Molded Waldorf Salad (page 55) and Hot Fruit Compote (page 93).

6 to 8 servings.

Note: If turkey roast is in cello-bag and directions call for cooking in bag, do not remove. With kitchen scissors, snip a small X in top of bag; pour wine mixture through funnel into bag.

Substitution

 For wine: 1 cup apple juice.

TURKEY ROAST ORANGE

Bake 2-pound frozen turkey roast as directed on package except—20 minutes before end of roasting time, remove roast to ovenproof platter. Spread ½ cup orange marmalade on roast; bake uncovered 20 minutes longer.

We like this with Green and White Salad (page 53) and Rice Medley (page 74).

6 servings.

ROAST HALF TURKEY

Prepare half turkey as directed for Roast Turkey (page 39) except—skewer skin to meat along cut edges to prevent shrinking from meat during roasting. Prepare 1 package (7 ounces) dry herbed stuffing as directed. On aluminum foil-covered rack in shallow roasting pan, mound stuffing on foil in shape of cavity. Place turkey skin side up on stuffing. Press foil up around base of turkey. Insert meat thermometer in thickest part of breast. Be sure it does not touch bone. Roast until meat thermometer registers 185°—approximately 3 to 3½ hours for an 8- to 10-pound half turkey, approximately 3½ to 4 hours for a 10- to 12-pound half turkey.

PINEAPPLE BRAISED DRUMSTICKS

 1 package (about 2½ pounds) frozen
  turkey drumsticks, thawed
 2 tablespoons shortening
  Salt and pepper
 1 cup pineapple juice
 ½ cup pineapple juice
 2 tablespoons flour

In large skillet, brown drumsticks slowly in shortening. Drain off fat. Season with salt and pepper and pour on 1 cup pineapple juice. Cover tightly; simmer 2 to 2½ hours or until tender, turning occasionally. Remove drumsticks and keep warm.

In tightly covered jar, shake ½ cup pineapple juice and flour; stir slowly into hot liquid. Heat to boiling, stirring constantly. Boil and stir 1 minute. Serve gravy with drumsticks.

Menu suggestions: spinach, Cucumber Relish Mold (page 55) and Coconut Rice (page 73).

4 servings.

VARIATION

■ *Deluxe Turkey Drumsticks:* Stir in 1 can (13½ ounces) pineapple chunks, drained, and 1 green pepper, thinly sliced, 15 minutes before end of cooking time.

Pictured at right:
Herbed Turkey Roast and Deluxe Turkey
Drumsticks—turkey treatments for today.

SLICED TURKEY AND DRESSING BAKE

 1 **package (7 ounces) dry herbed stuffing mix**
 1 **package (28 ounces) frozen turkey slices in gravy**

Heat oven to 400°. Prepare stuffing as directed on package; pat into greased baking dish, 11½ × 7½ × 1½ inches. Remove frozen turkey and gravy from foil; place on stuffing. Bake uncovered 1 hour.

VARIATION

■ *Sliced Beef and Dressing Bake:* Substitute 1 package (24 ounces) frozen beef slices in gravy for the turkey slices in gravy.

TURKEY DIVAN

 2 **packages (10 ounces each) frozen broccoli spears**
 6 **slices turkey, about ¼ inch thick**
 6 **slices process American cheese**
 1 **can (10¾ ounces) condensed cream of mushroom soup**
 ⅓ **cup milk**
 1 **can (3 ounces) French fried onions**

Heat oven to 350°. Rinse broccoli with small amount of running cold water to separate and remove ice crystals; drain. Arrange broccoli in ungreased baking dish, 11½ × 7½ × 1½ inches. (If broccoli stems are more than ½ inch in diameter, cut lengthwise in half.)

Top broccoli with turkey and cheese slices. Cover with mixture of soup and milk. Bake uncovered 25 minutes. Sprinkle with onions; bake 5 minutes longer.

4 to 6 servings.

Substitutions

For broccoli: 2 packages (10 ounces each) frozen asparagus spears.

For sliced turkey: 1½ to 2 cups cut-up cooked turkey.

VARIATION

■ *Chicken Divan:* Substitute 1½ to 2 cups cut-up cooked chicken for the turkey slices.

WILD RICE AND TURKEY CASSEROLE

 2 **cups cut-up cooked turkey**
 1 **package (6 ounces) seasoned long grained and wild rice**
 1 **can (10¾ ounces) condensed cream of mushroom soup**
 ⅓ **cup milk**
 ¼ **cup chopped onion**
 ½ **teaspoon salt**
 2¼ **cups boiling water**

Heat oven to 350°. Mix all ingredients in ungreased 2-quart casserole. Cover tightly; bake about 50 minutes or until rice is tender. Uncover; bake 10 to 15 minutes longer.

We like Green and White Salad (page 53) with this easy oven casserole.

6 servings.

VARIATION

■ *Wild Rice and Chicken Casserole:* Substitute 2 cups cut-up cooked chicken for the turkey.

FRUITED TURKEY SALAD

1½ **cups cut-up cooked turkey**
 1 **can (8¼ ounces) green grapes, drained**
 1 **can (5 ounces) water chestnuts, drained and chopped**
 1 **can (11 ounces) mandarin orange segments, drained**
 ½ **cup mayonnaise or salad dressing**
 ½ **teaspoon salt**
 ¼ **teaspoon curry powder**

Combine turkey, grapes, water chestnuts and orange segments. Mix remaining ingredients; toss with turkey mixture.

So pretty when served in a bowl lined with greens and garnished with toasted almonds.

3 or 4 servings.

Substitution

For canned grapes: 1 cup fresh seedless green grapes.

VARIATION

■ *Fruited Chicken Salad:* Substitute 1½ cups cut-up cooked chicken for the turkey.

Fish and Seafood

BAKED FISH

2 pounds fish fillets or steaks
  Salt and pepper
2 tablespoons lemon juice
1 teaspoon grated onion
¼ cup butter or margarine, melted

Heat oven to 350°. If fillets are large, cut into serving pieces. Season with salt and pepper. Mix lemon juice, onion and butter; dip fish into butter mixture.

Arrange fish in greased baking pan, 9 × 9 × 2 inches. Pour remaining butter mixture on fish. Bake uncovered 25 to 30 minutes or until fish flakes easily with fork. Sprinkle with paprika if you like.

About 6 servings.

GOLDEN SOLE

1 package (16 ounces) frozen sole fillets
  Salt and pepper
1 tablespoon butter or margarine
1 package (1¾ ounces) hollandaise
  sauce mix
1 can (19 ounces) asparagus spears, drained

Thaw fillets just until they can be separated. Heat oven to 475°. Arrange fish in ungreased baking dish, 11½ × 7½ × 1½ inches, leaving space in center of dish. Season fish with salt and pepper and dot with butter. Bake uncovered 15 minutes.

While fish bakes, prepare hollandaise sauce as directed on package. Remove fish from oven; arrange asparagus in center of dish. Pour hollandaise sauce on asparagus. Bake 5 minutes or until heated through.

Serve with Country-style Waldorf Salad (page 56), a green vegetable and Dill Mashed Potatoes (page 65). Strawberry Cream (page 100) is the beverage-dessert.

3 or 4 servings.

HALIBUT WITH VEGETABLES

1½ to 2 pounds halibut fillets
1 teaspoon salt
¼ teaspoon pepper
¼ teaspoon paprika
2 carrots
3 stalks celery
6 green onions
1 teaspoon salt
¼ cup butter or margarine
1 tablespoon lemon juice

Heat oven to 350°. Arrange fish in ungreased baking pan, 13 × 9 × 2 inches. Season with 1 teaspoon salt, the pepper and paprika.

Cut carrots, celery and onions (with tops) into 1-inch lengths. Place in blender; add water to cover. Chop, watching carefully. Drain thoroughly. (Or carrots can be shredded and celery and onions finely chopped by hand).

Spread vegetables on fish; season with 1 teaspoon salt. Dot with butter and sprinkle with lemon juice. Cover tightly; bake 30 minutes or until fish flakes easily with fork.

Herbed Zucchini (page 64) and Creamy Blackeye Peas (page 63) round out the main dish.

6 servings.

Note: This dish can be prepared ahead of time, refrigerated and baked later. Increase the baking time 15 minutes.

POACHED FISH

1 medium onion, sliced
3 slices lemon
3 sprigs parsley
1 bay leaf
1 teaspoon salt
2 peppercorns
1 pound fish fillets

Pour water (1½ inches) into large skillet; add onion, lemon slices, parsley, bay leaf, salt and peppercorns and heat to boiling.

Arrange fish in single layer in skillet. Cover tightly; simmer 4 to 6 minutes or until fish flakes easily.

2 or 3 servings.

BROILED FISH

2 pounds fish fillets or steaks,
about 1 inch thick
1 teaspoon salt
⅛ teaspoon pepper
¼ cup butter or margarine, melted

Set oven control at broil and/or 550°. Grease broiler pan and place in oven to heat. If fillets are large, cut into serving pieces. Season with salt and pepper. If fish has not been skinned, arrange skin side up in broiler pan; brush with some of the butter.

Broil fish 2 to 3 inches from heat 5 to 8 minutes or until light brown. Brush with butter; turn carefully and brush again. Broil 5 to 8 minutes longer or until fish flakes easily with fork.

6 servings.

VARIATION

■ *Broiled Fish Italiano:* Omit salt, pepper and butter; brush fish with ¼ cup Italian salad dressing during broiling.

PARSLEYED FISH BROIL

1½ to 2 pounds fish fillets or steaks,
¾ to 1 inch thick
1 teaspoon salt
⅛ teaspoon pepper
½ cup butter or margarine, melted
¼ cup lemon juice
2 tablespoons snipped parsley

Set oven control at broil and/or 550°. Grease rack in broiler pan and place in oven to heat. Season fish with salt and pepper. Mix remaining ingredients; brush some of the butter mixture on fish.

Broil fish 2 to 3 inches from heat 3 to 5 minutes or until brown. Brush with butter mixture; turn carefully and brush again. Broil 3 to 5 minutes longer or until fish flakes easily with fork. Serve with remaining butter mixture.

Suggested go-withs: Sautéed Spinach (page 63), Frozen Cocktail Salad (page 55) and Potatoes O'Brien (page 66).

6 servings.

CRISPY FISH STICKS

1 package (16 ounces) frozen fish sticks
¼ cup tomato French salad dressing
½ to ¾ teaspoon barbecue spice
1 tablespoon lemon juice
½ teaspoon prepared mustard

Arrange frozen fish sticks on ungreased baking sheet. Mix remaining ingredients; brush on fish. Bake or broil as directed on package.

Serve with Dilled Peas and Cauliflower (page 62) and an orange and grapefruit salad.

4 or 5 servings.

LIME-GLAZED FISH STICKS

1 package (8 ounces) frozen fish sticks
¼ cup lime marmalade, melted
2 tablespoons lime juice

Bake fish sticks as directed on package for oven method except—blend marmalade and juice; spoon onto fish sticks for the last 5 minutes of baking.

Peas and Almonds (page 62) are great with this quick fish fix-up.

3 servings.

VARIATION

■ *Orange-glazed Fish Sticks:* Substitute ¼ cup orange marmalade, melted, for the lime marmalade and 2 tablespoons lemon juice for the lime juice.

FISH STICKS
WITH MUSHROOMS AND PECANS

1 package (8 ounces) frozen fish sticks
1 can (4 ounces) mushrooms stems and
pieces, drained
¼ cup chopped onion
¼ cup butter or margarine, melted
¼ cup chopped pecans

Arrange frozen fish sticks in jelly roll pan, 15½ × 10½ × 1 inch. Mix remaining ingredients and spoon onto fish sticks. Bake as directed on package.

Nice with our colorful Pineapple-Cheese Mold (page 55).

3 servings.

PANFRIED FISH

2 pounds fish fillets, steaks or
  pan-dressed fish
1 teaspoon salt
⅛ teaspoon pepper
1 egg
1 tablespoon water
1 cup all-purpose flour
  Shortening (part butter)

If fillets are large, cut into serving pieces. Season with salt and pepper. Beat egg and water slightly. Dip fish into egg, then coat with flour. Melt shortening (⅛ inch) in skillet; fry fish over medium heat, about 10 minutes.

4 to 6 servings.

Substitution

For flour: 1 cup buttermilk baking mix, cornmeal or grated Parmesan cheese.

VARIATION

■ *Fish Almondine:* Brown ¼ cup butter or margarine in small skillet; stir in ¼ cup toasted slivered blanched almonds, ¼ teaspoon salt and 2 teaspoons lemon juice. Just before serving, top fish with almond butter.

OVEN-FRIED FILLETS

2 pounds fish fillets or steaks
1 tablespoon salt
½ cup milk
1 cup dry bread crumbs
¼ cup butter or margarine, melted

Heat oven to 500°. If fillets are large, cut into serving pieces. Stir salt into milk. Dip fish into milk, then coat with bread crumbs. Arrange in well-greased baking pan, 13 × 9 × 2 inches.

Pour butter on fish. Place pan on rack slightly above middle of oven; bake uncovered 10 to 12 minutes or until fish flakes easily with fork.

6 servings.

HERBED SALMON STEAKS

Pictured on page 5.

3 packages (12 ounces each) frozen
  salmon steaks
¼ cup lemon juice
2 tablespoons butter or margarine, melted
2 teaspoons marjoram leaves
2 teaspoons onion salt
½ teaspoon seasoned pepper
  Paprika
  Lemon wedges
  Snipped parsley

Heat oven to 450°. Arrange frozen salmon steaks in greased baking pan, 13 × 9 × 2 inches. Mix lemon juice, butter, marjoram leaves, onion salt and seasoned pepper; brush on fish. Bake uncovered 35 minutes or until fish flakes easily with a fork. Sprinkle with paprika; garnish with lemon wedges and parsley.

Menu mates: Crunchy Creamy Spinach (page 63), sliced tomatoes and potato salad.

6 servings.

SCALLOP CASSEROLE

1 package (12 ounces) frozen scallops,
  thawed
¾ cup light cream (20%) or half-and-half
1 cup dry bread crumbs
½ cup butter or margarine, melted
2 teaspoons celery seed
1 teaspoon salt
¼ teaspoon pepper
  Paprika

Heat oven to 375°. If scallops are large, cut into 1½-inch pieces. Remove any shell particles and wash scallops. Arrange in greased baking dish, 11½ × 7½ × 1½ inches.

Pour about half the cream on scallops. Mix bread crumbs, butter and seasonings; sprinkle on scallops. Pour on remaining cream (liquid should come about ¾ of the way up on scallops). Sprinkle with paprika. Bake uncovered 25 to 30 minutes.

4 servings.

Substitution

For frozen scallops: ¾ pound fresh scallops.

Creamy Shrimp and Peas

Skillet Paella

JIFFY LOBSTER NEWBURG

- **1 can (5½ ounces) lobster, drained**
- **1 can (10¾ ounces) condensed cream of shrimp soup**
- **¼ cup milk**
- **3 tablespoons sherry**
- **2 or 3 slices toast**

Break lobster meat into pieces. Heat soup and milk, stirring occasionally. Add lobster; cook over low heat until heated through. Stir in wine. Serve on hot toast.

2 or 3 servings.

VARIATION

■ *Shrimp Newburg:* Substitute 1 can (4½ or 5 ounces) shrimp, rinsed and drained, for the lobster.

SKILLET PAELLA

- **1 package (12 ounces) frozen peeled shrimp**
- **1 can (7 to 8 ounces) minced clams**
- **1 can (5 ounces) boned chicken**
- **1 can (16 ounces) tomatoes**
- **1 package (10 ounces) frozen green peas, broken apart**
- **2 cups uncooked instant rice**
- **2 tablespoons instant minced onion**
- **1 teaspoon paprika**
- **1 teaspoon instant chicken bouillon**
- **¼ teaspoon cayenne red pepper**
- **⅛ teaspoon saffron**

Rinse frozen shrimp under running cold water to remove ice crystals. Stir together all ingredients in large skillet. Heat to boiling, stirring occasionally. Reduce heat; simmer 5 minutes. Remove skillet from heat. Cover tightly; let stand 10 minutes.

4 or 5 servings.

Substitutions

For frozen shrimp: 2 cans (4½ ounces each) jumbo shrimp, drained.

For canned chicken: ½ cup cubed cooked chicken.

For tomatoes: 1 can (16 ounces) stewed tomatoes.

For instant onion: ⅓ cup minced onion.

For instant bouillon: 1 chicken bouillon cube.

CREAMY SHRIMP AND PEAS

1 package (7 ounces) frozen peeled shrimp
1 can (10¾ ounces) condensed
   cream of shrimp soup
1 package (10 ounces) frozen green peas
2 tablespoons pasteurized process cheese
   spread
2 tablespoons sherry
4 baked patty shells

Rinse frozen shrimp under running cold water to remove ice crystals. Heat shrimp, soup and peas to boiling. Boil and stir 5 minutes. Stir in cheese spread and sherry; cook, stirring until cheese is melted. Serve in patty shells.

Molded Waldorf Salad (page 55) adds color to the meal.

4 servings.

Substitutions

For sherry: 1 tablespoon plus 1 teaspoon sherry flavoring.

For patty shells: Toast points.

TUNA AND RICE MELANGE

1 small onion, thinly sliced
1 tablespoon salad oil
1 package (10 ounces) frozen
   mixed vegetables
½ cup water
3 cups cooked rice (without salt)
2 cans (6½ ounces each) tuna, drained
1 cup thinly sliced celery
¼ cup soy sauce

In large skillet, cook and stir onion in oil until tender. Add frozen vegetables and water; heat to boiling. Reduce heat. Cover tightly; simmer 5 to 10 minutes or until vegetables are tender. Stir in remaining ingredients; heat through.

6 to 8 servings.

TUNA-NOODLE DINNER

1 package (5.5 ounces) noodles almondine
1 can (6½ ounces) tuna, drained
1 package (10 ounces) frozen mixed
   vegetables, broken apart

Heat oven to 350°. Prepare noodles almondine as directed on package for oven method except—stir in tuna and vegetables. Cover and bake about 25 minutes or until noodles and vegetables are tender. Stir before serving; garnish with Almonds.

This complete meal-in-a-dish needs only the crunch of celery sticks.

4 servings.

Substitution

For frozen vegetables: 1 cup cooked vegetable or mixed vegetables.

SALMON PUFF

2 cans (16 ounces each) salmon,
   drained (reserve liquid)
   About ¾ cup milk
2 eggs, slightly beaten
3 cups coarse cracker crumbs
¼ cup frozen chopped onion
1 teaspoon lemon pepper
¼ teaspoon salt

Heat oven to 350°. Flake salmon, removing bone and skin. Add enough milk to reserved salmon liquid to measure 1½ cups. Mix all ingredients. Pour into greased 2-quart casserole. Bake uncovered 45 minutes. Garnish with lemon twists or wedges.

We like this light, fluffy casserole with Best Tossed Salad (page 53) and Classic Bean Casserole (page 58)—baked in the same oven. Blender Orange-Raisin Cake (page 79) is the dessert choice.

6 to 8 servings.

Substitutions

For frozen onion: ¼ cup chopped onion.

For lemon pepper: 1 teaspoon lemon juice and ¼ teaspoon seasoned pepper.

Cheese, Eggs and Beans

CHEESE-SPINACH SOUFFLÉ

1 package (12 ounces) frozen
   spinach soufflé, thawed
2 packages (12 ounces each) frozen
   cheese soufflé, thawed

Heat oven to 350°. Butter 8-cup soufflé dish or 2-quart casserole. (If using soufflé dish, make a 4-inch band of triple thickness aluminum foil 2 inches longer than circumference of dish; butter one side. Extend depth of dish by securing foil band, buttered side in, around outside top of dish.)

Pour spinach soufflé into soufflé dish. Top with cheese soufflés. Bake 1 hour or until knife inserted halfway between edge and center comes out clean. Serve immediately. Carefully remove foil band and divide soufflé into sections with 2 forks.

Let the soufflé star for company. Serve with Artichokes and Peas (page 58) and Sesame Rye Fingers (page 68). Offer Cookie Refrigerator Dessert (page 97) for the finale.

5 or 6 servings.

JIFFY CHEESE FONDUE

1 clove garlic
2 cans (11 ounces each) condensed
   Cheddar cheese soup
½ cup dry white wine
   French bread

Rub cut clove of garlic around the inside of an earthenware fondue pot. Heat cheese soup and wine. Pour into fondue pot and keep hot over low heat. Use long-handled forks to spear 1-inch cubes of French bread, then dip and swirl in fondue.

Try other dippers for the fondue—cubes of cooked ham, cherry tomatoes, avocado chunks.

4 servings.

HAM AND CHEESE OVEN OMELET

8 eggs
1 cup milk
½ teaspoon seasoned salt
1 package (3 ounces) thin-sliced ham
1 cup shredded Cheddar cheese (4 ounces)
1 tablespoon instant minced onion

Heat oven to 325°. Beat eggs, milk and seasoned salt. Tear ham in small pieces into egg mixture. Stir in cheese and onion.

Pour into greased baking dish, 11½ × 7½ × 1½ or 8 × 8 × 2 inches. Bake uncovered 40 to 45 minutes or until omelet is set and top is golden brown.

4 to 6 servings.

Note: Remember this for a late-evening supper. Prepare mixture ahead of time and refrigerate until needed.

Substitutions

For ham: 1 package (3 ounces) thin-sliced corned beef or dried beef.

For Cheddar cheese: 1 cup shredded mozzarella, Swiss or other cheese.

For instant onion: 3 tablespoons minced onion.

PUFFY CHEESE BAKE

4 slices bread, buttered
2 eggs
1 cup half-and-half
2 tablespoons butter or margarine, melted
½ teaspoon salt
½ teaspoon dry mustard
¼ teaspoon paprika
   Dash cayenne red pepper
1½ cups shredded process American cheese (6 ounces)

Heat oven to 350°. Butter baking dish, 8 × 8 × 2 inches. Cut each slice of bread diagonally into 4 triangles. Line bottom and sides of baking dish with bread triangles. (For a crown effect, place 8 triangles upright against sides of dish. Arrange remaining triangles on bottom of dish).

Beat eggs slightly; add remaining ingredients and mix well. Pour mixture into baking dish. Bake uncovered 30 to 40 minutes.

4 servings.

PIZZA RICE

12 slices bacon, diced
   Cooked instant rice (enough for
   4 servings)
1½ cups shredded Cheddar cheese
   (6 ounces)
¼ cup instant minced onion
2 tablespoons dried green pepper
1 can (10½ ounces) pizza sauce

Fry bacon until crisp; drain off fat. Stir in rice and cheese; sprinkle with onion and green pepper. Pour sauce on rice. Cover tightly; cook over low heat until cheese melts, about 10 minutes.

4 to 6 servings.

Substitutions

For instant rice: 2 cups cooked rice.
For instant onion: 1 large onion, chopped.
For dried green pepper: ⅓ cup chopped green pepper.

EGGS CONTINENTAL

½ cup dry bread crumbs
1 tablespoon butter or margarine, melted
4 hard-cooked eggs, sliced
3 slices bacon, diced
1 cup dairy sour cream
1 tablespoon milk
1 tablespoon instant minced onion
½ teaspoon salt
¼ teaspoon paprika
⅛ teaspoon pepper
½ cup shredded Cheddar cheese

Heat oven to 350°. Toss bread crumbs in melted butter; divide among 4 buttered 10-ounce casseroles or baking dishes. Layer egg slices on crumbs.

Fry bacon until crisp; remove bacon and drain. Stir together bacon, sour cream, milk, onion and seasonings; spoon onto eggs. Top with cheese. Bake uncovered 10 to 15 minutes or until cheese is melted.

Buttered Brussels sprouts and rye toast make good go-withs.

4 servings.

Substitution

For instant onion: 3 tablespoons minced onion.

EGG FOO YONG

2 tablespoons salad oil
3 eggs
1 cup bean sprouts, drained
½ cup chopped cooked pork
2 tablespoons chopped onion
1 tablespoon soy sauce
   Sauce (below)

Heat oil in large skillet. Beat eggs until thick; stir in bean sprouts, pork, onion and soy sauce.

Pour ¼ cup mixture at a time into skillet; with broad spatula, push cooked egg up over meat to form a patty. When patties are set, turn to brown other side. Serve hot with Sauce.

5 servings.

SAUCE

1 teaspoon cornstarch
1 teaspoon sugar
1 teaspoon vinegar
2½ tablespoons soy sauce
½ cup water

Mix all ingredients in small saucepan. Cook, stirring constantly, until mixture thickens and boils. Boil and stir 1 minute.

CREAMED HAM AND EGGS

3 tablespoons butter or margarine
3 tablespoons flour
½ teaspoon dry mustard
¼ teaspoon salt
⅛ teaspoon pepper
2¼ cups milk
1 cup diced cooked ham
4 hard-cooked eggs, quartered
   Buttered toast

Melt butter in large saucepan over low heat. Blend in flour and seasonings. Cook over low heat, stirring until mixture is smooth and bubbly. Remove from heat. Stir in milk. Heat to boiling, stirring constantly. Boil and stir 1 minute. Gently stir in ham and eggs; heat through. Serve hot on toast.

6 servings.

Substitution

For toast: Toast cups, biscuits or hot fluffy rice.

CHEDDAR EGG BAKE

6 eggs, slightly beaten
1 cup shredded Cheddar cheese (4 ounces)
½ cup milk
2 tablespoons soft butter or margarine
1 teaspoon prepared mustard
½ teaspoon salt
¼ teaspoon pepper

Heat oven to 325°. Mix all ingredients. Pour into ungreased baking pan, 8 × 8 × 2 inches. Bake 25 to 30 minutes or until eggs are set.

6 servings.

COUNTRY CASSOULET

Pictured on page 5.

1 pound bulk pork sausage
1 cup sliced celery
½ cup chopped onion
½ cup chopped green pepper
⅛ teaspoon instant minced garlic
1 teaspoon salt
1 can (16 ounces) pork and beans
1 can (16 ounces) lima beans
1 can (6 ounces) tomato paste

Cook and stir sausage, celery, onion, green pepper, garlic and salt until meat is brown. Drain off fat. Stir in pork and beans (with sauce), lima beans (with liquid) and tomato paste. Simmer uncovered 10 minutes.

A tossed green salad—and lots of it—is all you need with this dinner in a dish.

5 or 6 servings.

LAZY MAN'S CHILI BEANS

4 slices bacon, diced
2 large onions, thinly sliced
2 cans (16 ounces each) kidney beans
1 can (15 ounces) chili without beans
¼ cup sugar
2 teaspoons salt
¼ teaspoon instant minced garlic

Fry bacon in large skillet until golden. Stir in onions; cook and stir until onion is tender. Stir in remaining ingredients. Simmer uncovered 25 to 30 minutes.

6 to 8 servings.

Substitution

For instant garlic: 2 cloves garlic, minced.

SPEEDY BAKED BEANS

2 cans (20 ounces each) baked beans (with pork)
¼ cup imitation bacon
¼ cup chili sauce
1 tablespoon instant minced onion
1 teaspoon prepared mustard

Heat oven to 350°. Combine all ingredients in greased 1½-quart casserole. Bake uncovered 45 minutes or until bubbly.

6 servings.

Substitution

For instant onion: 3 tablespoons minced onion.

Pictured at right:
TOP
  Cheese Potato Casserole
  Snow Peas and Carrot Nuggets
  Saucy Spaghetti and Sprouts
CENTER
  Broccoli 'n Chips
  Best Tossed Salad
  Rice Medley
BOTTOM
  Twin Pan Rolls (Parmesan)
  Sweet and Sour Beets
  Molded Waldorf Salad

Serve-Withs and Side Dishes

Salads

BOTTLED SALAD DRESSING FIX-UPS

Add the homemade touch to bottled dressing ease with any of the following combinations:

For vegetable salads:
¼ cup oil and vinegar salad dressing and ¼ teaspoon savory leaves, crushed
¼ cup oil and vinegar salad dressing and ¼ teaspoon oregano leaves, crushed
¼ cup oil and vinegar salad dressing and ¼ teaspoon thyme leaves, crushed
¼ cup oil and vinegar salad dressing and ¼ teaspoon chili powder

For cottage cheese salads:
¼ cup creamy French salad dressing and 1 tablespoon pickle sandwich spread
¼ cup creamy sour cream salad dressing and 1 teaspoon horseradish
¼ cup creamy blue cheese salad dressing and 1 tablespoon catsup or chili sauce
¼ cup creamy blue cheese salad dressing and ⅛ teaspoon curry powder (also good on fruit)

For fruit salads:
¼ cup creamy blue cheese salad dressing and 1 tablespoon apricot preserves
¼ cup creamy blue cheese salad dressing and 2 tablespoons creamy French salad dressing
¼ cup fruit salad dressing and ¼ teaspoon sesame seed

RUBY-RED FRUIT SALAD DRESSING

Beat ½ cup currant jelly and ¼ cup oil and vinegar salad dressing with rotary beater.

¾ cup.

Substitution

For currant jelly: ½ cup cranberry jelly.

VEGETABLE SALAD DRESSINGS

Catsup Mayonnaise: Blend ½ cup mayonnaise and ¼ cup catsup.

Chili Mayonnaise: Blend ½ cup mayonnaise, ¼ cup chili sauce, 1 drop red pepper sauce and dash chili powder.

Fluffy Mayonnaise: Blend ½ cup mayonnaise and ¼ cup frozen whipped topping (thawed).

¾ cup.

CREAMY LEMON DRESSING

⅓ **cup frozen lemonade concentrate (thawed)**
⅓ **cup honey**
⅓ **cup dairy sour cream**
1 **teaspoon celery seed**

Beat all ingredients with rotary beater. Perfect for fruit salads.

¾ cup.

Substitution

For dairy sour cream: ⅓ cup salad oil.

For Gorgeous Greens

A little TLC please. The beautiful greens deserve it. Buy them crisp and fresh, of course; store them, covered, in the refrigerator. And think twice about tossing away the outer leaves; that's where the vitamins are at their best.

Wash greens only as you need them. And do put aside that knife. Greens were meant to be torn, not cut—unless you're serving wedges, or want shredded leaves for slaw.

Avoid the head lettuce rut. Make friends with the whole family of leafy greens: romaine, endive, escarole, watercress. Use them together—the dark and the light, the crisp and the tender—and create your own splendid setting for vegetable sparkers and your favorite dressing.

But before you add these final fillips, make sure the greens are cold and dry. Then pour on the dressing at the very last moment—just enough to coat the leaves lightly—and toss. But ever so gently; that's all they need.

BEST TOSSED SALAD

Pictured on page 51.

- 1 small head lettuce
- 1 small bunch leaf lettuce
- ½ small bunch endive
- ½ bag (10-ounce size) spinach
- ¼ cup oil and vinegar salad dressing

Into large salad bowl or plastic bag, tear greens into bite-size pieces (12 cups). Toss with salad dressing until greens are well coated. If you like, toss in 1 cup herb-seasoned croutons.

6 to 8 servings.

GREEN AND WHITE SALAD

- 1 small head lettuce
- ½ small bunch endive
- ½ small cauliflower
- 1 jar (6 ounces) marinated artichoke hearts, drained (reserve marinade)
- 12 pitted ripe olives
- 2 tablespoons tarragon vinegar
- 1 teaspoon salt
- 1 teaspoon instant minced garlic

Into large salad bowl, tear greens into bite-size pieces (about 8 cups). Break cauliflower into flowerets, cut artichoke hearts in half and slice olives; add to greens.

Sprinkle with reserved artichoke marinade; toss until greens glisten. Sprinkle with vinegar, salt and garlic; toss until greens are well coated.

6 to 8 servings.

Substitutions

For endive: 4 cups bite-size pieces spinach (4 ounces).

For instant garlic: 1 clove garlic, minced.

TOSSED SALAD WITH CLASSIC DRESSING

- 1 medium head lettuce
- 1 medium cucumber, cut into thin slices
- 8 cherry tomatoes, cut into halves
- 1 tablespoon plus 1 teaspoon salad oil
- ½ teaspoon salt
  Dash garlic powder
  Dash pepper
- 2 teaspoons wine vinegar

Into salad bowl, tear lettuce into bite-size pieces. Add cucumber slices and tomato halves to salad bowl.

Sprinkle with oil; toss until lettuce glistens. Season with salt, garlic powder and pepper. Sprinkle with vinegar; toss until lettuce is well coated.

4 servings.

Note: For a pretty effect, run tines of fork down side of cucumber before slicing.

BLENDER COLESLAW

- ½ medium cabbage
- 1 small onion
- ⅔ cup dairy sour cream
- ¼ cup mayonnaise or salad dressing
- ½ teaspoon salt
- ½ teaspoon dry mustard
  Dash pepper

Cut cabbage into 2-inch pieces. Quarter onion. Place half the cabbage in blender; add water to cover. Chop, watching carefully. Drain thoroughly. Repeat with remaining cabbage and the onion. (Or vegetables can be shredded or finely chopped by hand.) Mix vegetables, sour cream, mayonnaise, salt, mustard and pepper. Chill.

6 to 8 servings.

VARIATIONS

- *Dill Slaw:* Add ½ teaspoon dill weed.

- *Herbed Slaw:* Omit mustard and pepper; add 1 teaspoon celery seed and ½ teaspoon chervil leaves.

- *Pineapple-Marshmallow Slaw:* Omit onion; stir in 1 can (13¼ ounces) pineapple chunks, drained and cut in half, 1 cup miniature marshmallows and 1 tablespoon lemon juice.

GREEN AND GOLD SALAD

　1 **package (10 ounces) frozen green peas**
　½ **cup shredded natural Cheddar cheese**
　2 **tablespoons chopped onion**
　2 **tablespoons mayonnaise or salad dressing**
　1½ **teaspoons prepared mustard**
　¼ **teaspoon salt**
　　Crisp salad greens

Rinse peas with small amount of running cold water to separate and remove ice crystals; drain. Mix all ingredients except salad greens. Serve salad on greens.

4 or 5 servings.

Substitution

　For frozen green peas; 1 can (8 ounces) green peas, drained.

MARINATED CUCUMBER SALAD

　1 **medium cucumber**
　1 **small onion**
　½ **cup vinegar**
　½ **cup water**
　2 **tablespoons sugar**
　¼ **teaspoon salt**
　　Crisp salad greens

Run tines of fork lengthwise down side of unpared cucumber. Thinly slice cucumber and onion. Mix vinegar, water, sugar and salt; pour on cucumber and onion in glass bowl. Cover; refrigerate at least 2 hours. Drain and serve on salad greens.

4 to 6 servings.

BRUSSELS AND CARROTS SALAD

　½ **cup oil and vinegar salad dressing**
　1 **package (10 ounces) frozen**
　　Brussels sprouts
　1 **can (16 ounces) sliced carrots, drained**

In covered saucepan, heat salad dressing and Brussels sprouts to boiling. Reduce heat; cover and simmer 8 minutes. Add carrots; cook until Brussels sprouts are tender. Turn into serving dish. Cover; refrigerate at least 6 hours, stirring occasionally.

6 to 8 servings.

OKRA AND TOMATO SALAD

　1 **package (10 ounces) frozen whole okra**
　1 **tomato, chopped**
　½ **cup sliced celery**
　1 **teaspoon cream-style horseradish**
　3 **tablespoons oil and vinegar salad dressing**
　　Crisp salad greens

Cook okra as directed on package; drain and cut into ½-inch pieces. Mix all ingredients except salad greens. Cover; refrigerate at least 4 hours. Serve on salad greens.

4 or 5 servings.

BRIGHT BEAN SALAD

　1 **medium carrot**
　1 **can (15½ ounces) French-style**
　　green beans, drained
　2 **tablespoons chopped onion**
　⅛ **teaspoon salt**
　3 **tablespoons oil and vinegar salad dressing**

Cut carrot into 1-inch lengths; chop in blender, watching carefully. (Or carrot can be finely chopped by hand.) Mix all ingredients. Cover; refrigerate at least 4 hours.

4 servings.

Substitutions

　For canned green beans: 1 package (9 ounces) frozen French-style green beans, cooked and drained.

　For fresh onion: 1 tablespoon instant minced.

Yesterday's Vegetables—Today's Salads

You cooked too many peas yesterday? Great! You've got a headstart on a new salad: Marinate them in oil and vinegar with chopped green pepper, onion and celery for added flavor. Then garnish with pimiento to serve. Or if you have cooked cauliflowerets around, combine them wih tomato wedges and cucumber slices. Let the flavors mingle in French dressing; serve in lettuce cups. And don't let leftover cooked potatoes throw you. Soak them in the liquid of marinated artichoke hearts—along with the hearts, of course—for a very fancy salad. The marinating time for each leftover vegetable, and its new friends, should be about 4 hours, in the refrigerator.

CUCUMBER RELISH MOLD

Pictured on page 57.

- **1 package (3 ounces) lime-flavored gelatin**
- **1 medium cucumber**
- **2 celery stalks**
- **5 green onions**
- **½ teaspoon salt**

Prepare gelatin as directed on package except—decrease water to 1½ cups and chill until slightly thickened but not set.

Cut unpared cucumber lengthwise into quarters, then into 1½-inch lengths. Cut celery and onions into 1½-inch lengths. Place vegetables in blender; add water to cover. Chop, watching carefully. Drain thoroughly. (Or vegetables can be finely chopped by hand. Be sure to drain cucumber thoroughly.)

Stir vegetables and salt into gelatin. Pour into 4-cup mold or 6 individual molds. Chill until firm, at least 6 hours. For a festive touch, unmold on salad greens. A sour cream salad dressing offers an interesting contrast.

6 servings.

MOLDED WALDORF SALAD

Pictured on page 51.

- **1 cup boiling water**
- **1 package (3 ounces) lemon-flavored gelatin**
- **1 can (11 ounces) mandarin orange segments**
- **1 can (8¼ ounces) crushed pineapple**
- **1 medium apple, diced**
- **1 medium banana, sliced**
- **¼ cup nuts, coarsely chopped**

Pour boiling water on gelatin in large bowl, stirring until gelatin is dissolved. Stir in orange segments (with syrup), pineapple (with syrup), apple, banana and nuts.

Pour into 5-cup mold or 8 to 10 individual molds. Chill until firm. Serve with your favorite fruit salad dressing.

6 to 8 servings.

PINEAPPLE-CHEESE MOLD

- **1 cup boiling water**
- **1 package (3 ounces) lemon-flavored gelatin**
- **2 tablespoons lemon juice or vinegar**
- **1 can (8¼ ounces) crushed pineapple, drained (reserve syrup)**
- **1 cup shredded Cheddar cheese (4 ounces)**
- **1 cup whipping cream, whipped**

Pour boiling water on gelatin in large bowl, stirring until gelatin is dissolved. Add lemon juice and enough water to reserved pineapple syrup to measure 1 cup; stir into gelatin. Chill until slightly thickened but not set.

Stir in pineapple and cheese; fold in whipped cream. Pour into 4-cup mold or 8 individual molds. Chill until firm.

8 servings.

Substitution

For whipped cream: 1 envelope (about 2 ounces) dessert topping mix prepared as directed.

FROZEN COCKTAIL SALAD

- **2 cups dairy sour cream**
- **¾ cup sugar**
- **1 tablespoon plus 1 teaspoon lemon juice**
- **1 can (30 ounces) fruit cocktail, drained**
- **2 medium bananas, cut into ¼-inch slices**
- **½ cup coarsely chopped walnuts**
- **1 jar (10 ounces) maraschino cherries (¾ cup), halved**

Mix sour cream, sugar and lemon juice. Stir in fruit cocktail, bananas, nuts and cherries. Pour into 2 refrigerator trays. Freeze 24 hours or until firm. (Upright or chest freezers will freeze salad in about 2 hours.)

About 15 minutes before serving, remove trays from freezer and place in refrigerator. Cut each salad into 8 pieces, 2 × 2¼ inches. Stemmed red cherries make a bright garnish.

16 servings.

Note: This salad can be kept covered in freezer 3 to 4 weeks.

CINNAMON-APPLESAUCE SALAD

¼ to ½ cup red cinnamon candies
½ cup water
1 package (3 ounces) lemon-flavored gelatin
1½ cups applesauce

Heat cinnamon candies and water, stirring frequently, until candies are melted. Pour on gelatin in bowl, stirring until gelatin is dissolved. Stir in applesauce.

Pour into 3- or 4-cup mold or into baking pan 8 × 8 × 2 inches. Chill until firm. Try a garnish of cream cheese balls rolled in chopped nuts.

6 servings.

Note: For 12 servings, double amounts and pour into 6-cup mold or into baking pan, 13 × 9 × 2 inches.

AMBROSIA SALAD

1 can (11 ounces) mandarin orange segments, drained
1 medium unpared apple, chopped
2 medium bananas, sliced
¼ cup chopped dates (sugar rolled)
2 tablespoons fruit salad dressing
    Lettuce cups
    Plain or toasted coconut

Toss orange segments, apple, bananas, dates and fruit salad dressing. Serve in lettuce cups. Sprinkle salads with coconut.

4 to 5 servings.

SEEDLESS GRAPE SALAD

1 can (8¼ ounces) seedless grapes, drained
1 cup diced celery
½ cup maraschino cherries, halved
¼ cup coarsely chopped nuts
2 tablespoons fruit salad dressing
    Lettuce cups

Toss grapes, celery, cherries, nuts and fruit salad dressing. Serve in lettuce cups.

2 or 3 servings.

Substitution

For canned grapes: 1 cup fresh seedless green grapes.

ORANGE-CAULIFLOWER SALAD

Pictured at right.

2 cans (11 ounces each) mandarin orange segments, drained
2 cups uncooked cauliflowerets
¼ cup chopped green pepper
2 cups bite-size pieces spinach (about 2 ounces)
¼ cup French salad dressing
    Lettuce cups

Toss orange segments, cauliflowerets, green pepper, spinach and salad dressing. Serve in lettuce cups.

5 or 6 servings.

Substitution

For French salad dressing: Fruit salad dressing.

ORANGE AND ONION SALAD

2 cans (11 ounces each) mandarin orange segments, drained
3 tablespoons finely chopped onion
    Crisp salad greens

Toss orange segments and onion. Serve on salad greens. Nice with Roquefort dressing.

4 servings.

COUNTRY-STYLE WALDORF SALAD

Pictured at right.

2 cups diced unpared apple
1 cup diced celery
1 can (8¼ ounces) seedless grapes, drained
⅓ cup coarsely chopped nuts
4 cups bite-size pieces lettuce
½ cup mayonnaise or salad dressing

Toss all ingredients. Garnish with slices of red apple for added color.

4 to 6 servings.

Substitution

For canned grapes: 1 cup fresh seedless green grapes.

Pictured at right:
Orange-Cauliflower Salad, Country-style
Waldorf Salad and Cucumber Relish Mold

Vegetables

ARTICHOKES AND PEAS

1 package (10 ounces) frozen artichoke
  hearts
1 package (10 ounces) frozen green peas
¾ cup water
1 teaspoon salt
1 tablespoon butter or margarine, melted
1 tablespoon lemon juice

In covered saucepan, heat frozen vegetables, water
and salt to boiling. Reduce heat and cook until peas
and artichoke hearts are tender, 5 to 8 minutes;
drain. Turn into serving dish; pour butter and
lemon juice on vegetables.

4 or 5 servings.

ASPARAGUS WITH CHEESE SAUCE

1 package (10 ounces) frozen cut asparagus
½ can (11-ounce size) condensed Cheddar
  cheese soup (⅔ cup)
½ cup canned French fried onions

Cook asparagus as directed on package; drain. Return to saucepan. Stir in cheese soup; heat through.
Turn into serving dish; top with French fried
onions.

4 servings.

ASPARAGUS À LA POLONAISE

¼ cup seasoned croutons
1 tablespoon butter or margarine
2 cans (15 ounces each) cut asparagus
1 tablespoon butter or margarine, melted
1 hard-cooked egg, chopped

Cook and stir croutons in 1 tablespoon butter until
brown. Heat asparagus; drain. Turn asparagus into
serving dish; drizzle with melted butter and sprinkle with croutons and egg.

4 or 5 servings.

DELUXE BEAN CASSEROLE

2 packages (9 ounces each) frozen
  French-style green beans
1 can (15 ounces) bean sprouts, rinsed
  and drained
1 can (10¾ ounces) condensed cream of
  mushroom soup
1 tablespoon soy sauce
1 teaspoon salt
1 cup canned French fried onions

Heat oven to 350°. Rinse beans with small amount
of running cold water to separate and remove ice
crystals; drain. Mix all ingredients except onions
in ungreased 2-quart casserole. Bake uncovered
25 minutes. Top with onions; bake 5 minutes
longer.

6 to 8 servings.

VARIATION

■ *Classic Bean Casserole:* Omit bean sprouts and
soy sauce.

GREEN BEANS AND BACON

3 slices bacon
1 tablespoon chopped onion
⅛ teaspoon instant minced garlic
1 tablespoon soy sauce
1 can (16 ounces) French-style
  green beans, drained

Fry bacon until crisp; remove bacon and drain.
Drain off all but 2 teaspoons fat. Cook and stir onion
in fat until tender. Stir in remaining ingredients;
heat through. Turn beans into serving dish; crumble bacon on beans.

4 servings.

Substitutions

For instant garlic: 1 clove garlic, minced.
For French-style green beans: 1 can (16 ounces)
cut green beans, drained.

MUSHROOM ITALIAN GREEN BEANS

1 can (4 ounces) mushroom stems
  and pieces, drained (reserve liquid)
1 package (9 ounces) frozen Italian
  green beans
1 tablespoon butter or margarine
½ teaspoon salt

Add enough water to reserved mushroom liquid to measure ½ cup; pour into medium saucepan. Add mushrooms, beans, butter and salt; cook as directed on package or until beans are tender.

4 servings.

PERKY LIMA BEANS

1 package (10 ounces) frozen lima beans
2 tablespoons soft butter or margarine
1 teaspoon sugar
1 teaspoon dry mustard
1 teaspoon lemon juice
¼ teaspoon salt

Cook lima beans as directed on package; drain. Stir in remaining ingredients.

4 servings.

Substitution

For frozen lima beans: 1 can (15 ounces) lima beans, heated and drained.

HICKORY LIMAS

1 package (10 ounces) frozen lima beans
¼ cup pasteurized process cheese spread
  with hickory smoke flavor
2 tablespoons milk

Cook lima beans as directed on package; drain. Return to saucepan. Stir in cheese spread and milk; heat, stirring constantly, until cheese spread is melted and smooth.

4 servings.

Substitutions

For frozen lima beans: 1 can (15 ounces) lima beans, heated and drained.

For cheese spread: ¼ cup pasteurized process cheese spread with bacon or garlic.

SAVORY BEETS

1 can (16 ounces) whole or sliced beets
2 tablespoons butter or margarine
1 teaspoon salt
½ teaspoon savory
½ teaspoon basil

In covered saucepan, heat all ingredients to boiling. Reduce heat; simmer 10 minutes.

4 servings.

SWEET AND SOUR BEETS

Pictured on page 51.

1 jar (16 ounces) pickled beets, drained
  (reserve syrup)
1 tablespoon cornstarch
1 can (11 ounces) mandarin orange segments,
  drained

Blend reserved beet syrup and the cornstarch in medium saucepan. Cook, stirring constantly, until mixture thickens and boils. Boil and stir 1 minute. Stir in beets and orange segments; heat through.

4 servings.

Substitutions

For pickled beets and cornstarch: 1 jar (16 ounces) Harvard beets.

For mandarin orange segments: 1 can (8¼ ounces) pineapple chunks.

BROCCOLI ELEGANT

1 package (10 ounces) frozen broccoli
  spears
½ can (11-ounce size) condensed Cheddar
  cheese soup (⅔ cup)
3 tablespoons milk
2 tablespoons sliced ripe olives

Cook broccoli as directed on package; drain. Mix cheese soup and milk in saucepan. Stir in broccoli and olives; heat through.

4 servings.

BROCCOLI 'N CHIPS

Pictured on page 51.

- **1 package (10 ounces) frozen chopped broccoli**
- **¼ cup canned shoestring potatoes**
- **2 teaspoons lemon juice**

Cook broccoli as directed on package; drain. Turn into serving dish; top with shoestring potatoes and sprinkle with lemon juice.

4 servings.

SPROUTS SAUTÉ

- **1 package (10 ounces) frozen Brussels sprouts**
- **½ cup water**
- **1 teaspoon instant chicken bouillon**
- **½ medium onion, sliced and separated into rings**
- **2 tablespoons butter or margarine**

In covered saucepan, heat Brussels sprouts, water and bouillon to boiling. Reduce heat; cook 5 minutes. Stir in onion and butter; cook uncovered until onion is tender, about 5 minutes.

3 servings.

Substitution

For instant bouillon: 1 chicken bouillon cube.

BOHEMIAN CABBAGE

- **1 medium cabbage (about 1½ pounds), shredded (about 5 cups)**
- **¼ cup water**
- **1 tablespoon instant minced onion**
- **1 teaspoon salt**
- **½ teaspoon caraway seed**
- **¼ teaspoon pepper**
- **½ cup dairy sour cream**

Mix all ingredients except sour cream in skillet. Cover tightly; cook 5 minutes or until cabbage is crisp-tender. Stir in sour cream; heat through.

6 servings.

Substitution

For instant onion: 3 tablespoons minced onion.

HOT VEGETABLE RELISHES

- **1 can (16 ounces) whole carrots**
- **2 stalks celery, cut into ¼-inch diagonal slices (about 1 cup)**
- **½ cup sweet pickle sticks**
- **½ teaspoon salt**

Mix carrots (with liquid), celery, pickle sticks and salt in saucepan; heat through.

4 servings.

Substitution

For sweet pickle sticks: ½ cup drained watermelon pickles.

CARROTS BOUILLON

- **1 can (16 ounces) carrot slices**
- **2 teaspoons instant minced onion**
- **1 teaspoon instant beef bouillon**
- **1 bay leaf**

In covered saucepan, heat carrot slices (with liquid), onion, bouillon and bay leaf to boiling. Reduce heat; simmer 5 minutes.

4 servings.

Substitutions

For instant onion: 2 tablespoons minced onion.
For instant bouillon: 1 beef bouillon cube.

CAULIFLOWER AND BRUSSELS SPROUTS

- **1 package (10 ounces) cauliflower frozen in cheese sauce in cooking pouch**
- **1 package (10 ounces) frozen Brussels sprouts**
- **2 tablespoons crumble herb stuffing, if desired**

Cook each vegetable as directed on package. Drain Brussels sprouts and turn into serving dish. Pour cauliflower on sprouts; toss to mix. Sprinkle with stuffing.

5 or 6 servings.

Substitution

For Brussels sprouts: 1 package (10 ounces) frozen lima beans.

CREAMY CORN AND CUCUMBER

1 **package (1½ ounces) white sauce mix**
1 **teaspoon instant chicken bouillon**
1 **medium cucumber**
1 **can (17 ounces) whole kernel corn, drained**

Prepare white sauce as directed on package except—stir instant chicken bouillon into white sauce mix before adding milk.

Cut unpared cucumber lengthwise into quarters, then crosswise into 1-inch pieces. Stir cucumber and corn into white sauce; heat through.

5 servings.

CORN SESAME SAUTÉ

1 **tablespoon butter or margarine**
1 **clove garlic, crushed**
2 **tablespoons sesame seed**
½ **teaspoon salt**
¼ **teaspoon basil leaves**
⅛ **teaspoon pepper**
1 **can (12 ounces) vacuum-pack whole kernel corn**

In medium skillet, cook and stir all ingredients except corn over medium heat until sesame seed is toasted. Stir in corn; heat through.

4 servings.

OVEN-FRIED EGGPLANT

½ **cup seasoned crumbs**
1 **teaspoon salt**
1 **small eggplant (about 1 pound), pared**
1 **egg, slightly beaten**

Heat oven to 375°. Grease jelly roll pan, 15½ × 10½ × 1 inch. Mix seasoned crumbs and salt. Cut eggplant into ½-inch slices. Dip slices into egg, then coat with crumbs. Arrange in pan. Bake uncovered 15 minutes; turn and bake 15 minutes longer.

4 servings.

Substitution

For seasoned crumbs: ½ cup dry bread crumbs and ¼ teaspoon pepper.

Creamy Corn and Cucumber

Oven-fried Eggplant

HOLLANDAISE ONIONS

Prepare 1 package (about 1½ ounces) hollandaise sauce mix as directed. Stir in 2 cups frozen whole onions. Heat over medium heat, stirring frequently, until tender, about 7 minutes.

4 servings.

CREAMED ONIONS AND BROCCOLI

1 package (10 ounces) frozen
  small onions in cream sauce
1 package (10 ounces) frozen broccoli spears
1 tablespoon creamy peanut butter

Cook each vegetable as directed on package except—stir peanut butter into onions until sauce is smooth. Drain broccoli and turn into serving dish; pour onions over broccoli.

4 or 5 servings.

VARIATION

■ *Nutmeg Creamed Onions and Broccoli:* Omit peanut butter and stir in ⅛ teaspoon nutmeg.

BROILED ONIONS AND POTATOES

Shape aluminum foil into a broiler pan, $10 \times 7 \times 1\frac{1}{2}$ inches. Drain 1 can (16 ounces) whole onions and 1 can (16 ounces) whole potatoes. Place onions and potatoes in foil pan; dot with 1 or 2 tablespoons soft butter or margarine.

Set oven control at broil and/or 550°. Place pan on rack in broiler pan. Broil 3 inches from heat 4 minutes. Turn onions and potatoes; sprinkle with seasoned salt and paprika. Broil 3 minutes longer.

4 servings.

PEAS WITH CELERY AND ONION

1 package (10 ounces) frozen green peas
1 stalk celery, sliced (about ½ cup)
1 small onion, thinly sliced

Cook peas, celery and onion as directed on package for peas; drain. If desired, toss vegetables with 1 tablespoon soft butter or margarine.

3 or 4 servings.

PEAS AND ALMONDS

¼ cup slivered almonds
1 tablespoon butter or margarine
1 package (10 ounces) frozen green peas,
  broken apart
½ teaspoon salt

Cook and stir almonds in butter until light brown, 2 to 3 minutes. Stir in peas and salt. Cook, stirring frequently, until peas are tender, 5 to 7 minutes.

3 servings.

DILLED PEAS AND CAULIFLOWER

1 package (8 ounces) frozen green peas
  with cream sauce
1 package (10 ounces) frozen cauliflower
⅔ cup water
1 tablespoon butter or margarine
½ teaspoon dill weed

In covered saucepan, heat all ingredients to boiling. Reduce heat; cook 5 to 8 minutes or until cauliflower is tender. Remove from heat; stir until sauce is smooth.

4 servings.

SNOW PEAS AND CARROT NUGGETS

Pictured on page 51.

1 package (7 ounces) frozen Chinese
  pea pods
1 package (10 ounces) carrot nuggets
  frozen in butter sauce in cooking pouch
2 teaspoons lemon juice

Cook each vegetable as directed on package. Drain pea pods and turn into serving dish. Pour carrots and lemon juice on pea pods; toss.

4 servings.

Substitution

For pea pods: 1 package (9 ounces) frozen Italian green beans.

CREAMY BLACKEYE PEAS

1 package (10 ounces) frozen
  blackeye peas
4 slices bacon, diced
1 can (10¾ ounces) condensed
  cream of chicken soup
¼ teaspoon Worcestershire sauce
  Dash pepper

Cook peas and bacon as directed on package for peas; drain. Return to saucepan. Stir in remaining ingredients; heat through.

4 servings.

SPINACH AND BROCCOLI

1 package (10 ounces) frozen chopped
  spinach
1 package (10 ounces) frozen chopped
  broccoli
⅔ cup water
1 teaspoon salt
1 tablespoon butter or margarine, melted
1 tablespoon lemon juice

In covered saucepan, heat spinach, broccoli, water and salt to boiling, breaking vegetables apart with a fork. Reduce heat and cook 5 to 10 minutes or until vegetables are tender; drain. Turn into serving dish; toss with mixture of butter and lemon juice.

6 or 7 servings.

CRUNCHY CREAMY SPINACH

1 package (10 ounces) frozen chopped
  spinach
½ cup dairy sour cream
1 can (3 ounces) French fried onions

Cook spinach as directed on package; drain. Stir in sour cream. Turn into serving dish; top with onions.

4 servings.

SAUTÉED SPINACH

2 slices bacon, diced
1 small onion, thinly sliced
1 package (10 ounces) frozen chopped
  spinach, broken apart
½ teaspoon salt
  Dash pepper

In medium skillet, cook and stir bacon and onion until bacon is crisp. Stir in spinach, salt and pepper. Cover tightly; cook until spinach is tender, 5 to 8 minutes.

4 servings.

HONEY-CHILI SQUASH

¼ cup honey
2 tablespoons butter or margarine
½ to 1 teaspoon chili powder
½ teaspoon salt
1 can (15 ounces) squash
½ cup crumble herb stuffing

Heat oven to 350°. In small skillet, heat honey, butter, chili powder and salt jut to boiling, stirring occasionally. Reserve 2 tablespoons of the honey mixture; pour remainder into ungreased 1-quart casserole.

Blend squash into honey mixture in casserole. Toss stuffing with reserved honey mixture; sprinkle on squash. Bake uncovered 25 minutes or until topping is brown.

4 or 5 servings.

Substitutions

For honey and butter: ⅓ cup honey butter.

For canned squash: 1 package (12 ounces) frozen squash, thawed.

VARIATIONS

■ *Crusty Pecan Squash Bake:* Omit chili powder and stir in ⅛ teaspoon nutmeg. Substitute ½ cup coarsely chopped pecans for the herb stuffing.

■ *Marshmallow Puff Squash Bake:* Blend all the honey mixture into squash. Omit herb stuffing and sprinkle ½ cup miniature marshmallows on squash. Bake 30 minutes or until marshmallows are puffed and golden brown.

NUTTY BAKED SQUASH

2 **acorn squash (1 pound each)**
⅔ **cup graham cracker crumbs**
⅓ **cup coarsely chopped pecans**
⅓ **cup soft butter or margarine**
3 **tablespoons brown sugar**
¼ **teaspoon salt**
¼ **teaspoon nutmeg**

Heat oven to 400°. Cut each squash in half; remove seeds and fibers. Stir together remaining ingredients. Spoon ¼ of the crumb mixture into each squash half.

Arrange squash halves in ungreased baking dish, 11½ × 7½ × 1½ inches. Pour water (¼ inch) into baking dish. Cover; bake 35 to 40 minutes or until squash is tender.

4 servings.

Substitution

For graham cracker crumbs: ⅔ cup soda cracker crumbs.

HERBED ZUCCHINI

Cut 2 pounds unpared zucchini into 1-inch slices. Heat 1 inch salted water (½ teaspoon salt to 1 cup water) to boiling. Add zucchini. Cover tightly; heat to boiling. Reduce heat and cook until tender, 5 minutes; drain. Sprinkle with oregano.

4 servings.

ITALIAN-STYLE ZUCCHINI

1½ **pounds zucchini (about 6 small)**
1 **tablespoon Italian salad dressing mix**
¼ **cup salad oil**
Grated Parmesan cheese

Cut unpared zucchini lengthwise into ½-inch slices. Place slices in skillet; sprinkle with salad dressing mix and pour oil on zucchini. Cover tightly; cook until zucchini is tender, 12 to 16 minutes. Turn into serving dish; sprinkle with Parmesan cheese.

4 or 5 servings.

TOMATO-CABBAGE SKILLET

1 **teaspoon instant beef bouillon**
1 **can (16 ounces) tomato wedges in tomato juice, drained (reserve liquid)**
1 **small cabbage (about 1 pound), shredded (about 3 cups)**

In medium skillet, heat bouillon and reserved tomato liquid until bouillon is dissolved. Stir in cabbage. Cover tightly; cook about 3 minutes, stirring occasionally.

Stir in tomatoes. Cover; cook 3 to 5 minutes longer or until cabbage is crisp-tender and tomatoes are heated through.

4 servings.

Substitution

For instant bouillon: 1 beef bouillon cube.

BAKED STUFFED TOMATOES

6 **medium tomatoes (about 2 pounds)**
⅔ **cup crumble herb stuffing**
¼ **cup grated Parmesan cheese**
Parsley

Heat oven to 350°. Remove stem ends of tomatoes. Remove pulp, leaving ½-inch wall. Chop pulp; mix with stuffing and cheese.

Fill tomatoes with stuffing; arrange in ungreased baking dish, 8 × 8 × 2 inches. Bake 20 to 25 minutes or until tomatoes are heated through. Garnish with parsley.

6 servings.

BROILED TOMATOES

Wash 4 medium tomatoes (about 1½ pounds). Remove stem end from each; cut tomatoes crosswise in half.

Set oven control at broil and/or 550°. Dot each half with ½ teaspoon butter or margarine. Season with salt, pepper, basil leaves, oregano leaves or ground savory. Broil tomato halves cut side up 3 to 5 inches from heat 5 minutes or until tops are golden brown.

4 servings.

Potatoes

Starting with a mix...
MASHED POTATO STIR-INS

Prepare instant mashed potatoes as directed on package for 4 servings. Just before serving, try one of the following additions:

■ *Bacon:* Stir in 1 to 2 slices bacon, crisply fried and crumbled.

■ *Blue Cheese:* Stir in 1 to 1½ tablespoons crumbled blue cheese.

■ *Celery Seed:* Stir in ½ teaspoon celery seed.

■ *Chives:* Stir in 1 tablespoon snipped chives.

■ *Dill:* Stir in ¼ teaspoon dill weed.

■ *Green Pepper:* Stir in 1 tablespoon chopped green pepper.

■ *Mushroom:* Stir in 1 can (2 ounces) mushroom stems and pieces, drained.

■ *Mustard:* Stir in 1 to 1½ teaspoons prepared mustard.

■ *Olive:* Stir in 1½ tablespoons sliced pitted ripe olives or 1½ tablespoons sliced pimiento-stuffed olives.

■ *Pimiento:* Stir in 1 tablespoon chopped drained pimiento.

CHEESE POTATOES

Prepare instant mashed potatoes as directed on package for 8 servings except—omit butter; after stirring in potatoes, stir in 1 jar (5 ounces) pasteurized process sharp American cheese spread or flavored pasteurized Neufchâtel cheese spread (the latter is now available with a wide variety of added flavor sparkers).

Note: To prepare in oven, turn potato mixture into 1½-quart casserole. Bake uncovered in 350° oven 15 to 20 minutes or until heated through.

CHEESE POTATO CASSEROLE

Pictured on page 51.

    Instant mashed potatoes (enough for 8 servings)
½ teaspoon garlic salt
1 tablespoon snipped parsley
1 cup shredded sharp Cheddar cheese (4 ounces)
1½ cups cornflakes, crushed
2 tablespoons soft butter
½ teaspoon dry mustard
½ teaspoon paprika
¼ teaspoon salt

Heat oven to 325°. Prepare mashed potatoes as directed on package except—decrease salt to ½ teaspoon and add garlic salt. Stir in parsley and cheese. Turn into 1½-quart casserole. Stir remaining ingredients together; sprinkle on potatoes. Bake 20 minutes.

8 servings.

Starting with a mix...
AU GRATIN POTATO STIR-INS

Prepare 1 package (5.5 ounces) au gratin potatoes as directed except—before baking, try one of the following additions:

■ *Bacon:* Stir in 3 slices bacon, crisply fried and crumbled.

■ *Blue Cheese:* Stir in 2 tablespoons crumbled blue cheese.

■ *Dill:* Stir in ½ teaspoon dill weed.

■ *Green Onion:* Stir in 2 tablespoons thinly sliced green onion.

■ *Green Pepper:* Stir in ½ cup finely chopped green pepper.

■ *Mushroom:* Stir in 1 can (3 ounces) sliced mushrooms, drained.

■ *Mustard:* Stir in 1 tablespoon prepared mustard.

■ *Olive:* Stir in ¼ cup sliced pitted ripe olives or ½ cup sliced pimiento-stuffed olives.

■ *Pimiento:* Stir in 1 jar (2 ounces) sliced pimiento, drained.

Golden Potato Bake

Potatoes O'Brien

GOLDEN POTATO BAKE

½ cup cornflake crumbs
1 teaspoon salt
4 to 6 medium potatoes, pared
2 tablespoons butter or margarine, melted

Heat oven to 375°. Mix cornflake crumbs and salt. Brush potatoes with butter; coat with crumbs. Arrange in ungreased baking pan, 9×9×2 inches. Bake uncovered 1 to 1¼ hours or until potatoes are tender.

4 to 6 servings.

POTATOES O'BRIEN

⅓ cup chopped green pepper
2 tablespoons chopped pimiento
1 medium onion, chopped
¼ cup butter or margarine
1 package (16 ounces) frozen French fried
   potatoes, diced
1 teaspoon salt
⅛ teaspoon pepper

In large skillet, cook and stir green pepper, pimiento and onion in butter until onion is tender. Stir in potatoes, salt and pepper. Cook, stirring occasionally, until potatoes are brown and heated.

4 servings.

Substitution

For fresh green pepper: 2 tablespoons dried green pepper.

Starting with a mix...
SCALLOPED POTATO VARIATIONS

Prepare 1 package (5.5 ounces) scalloped potatoes as directed except—try one of the following easy variations:

■ *Blue Cheese:* Stir in 2 tablespoons crumbled blue cheese with the butter.

■ *Mushroom:* Stir in 1 can (3 ounces) sliced mushrooms, drained, or ½ cup sautéed sliced fresh mushrooms.

■ *Sour Cream:* Substitute ⅔ cup dairy sour cream for the milk.

4 to 6 servings.

CREAMY SCALLOPED POTATOES

1 package (5.5 ounces) scalloped potatoes
2 cups boiling water
1 can (10¾ ounces) condensed cream of
  celery soup
2 tablespoons butter or margarine

Heat oven to 400°. Empty potato slices into ungreased 1½-quart casserole; sprinkle with sauce mix. Stir in water, soup and butter. Bake uncovered 35 to 40 minutes.

4 to 6 servings.

Substitution

For cream of celery soup: 1 can (10¾ ounces) condensed cream of chicken soup or cream of mushroom soup.

SCALLOPED POTATO SALAD

1 package (5.5 ounces) scalloped potatoes
3 cups water
2 tablespoons salad oil
⅔ cup water
2 tablespoons white wine tarragon
  vinegar
½ cup mayonnaise or salad dressing
¼ teaspoon prepared mustard
½ cup diced celery
½ cup finely chopped onion
4 hard-cooked eggs, chopped
2 tablespoons snipped parsley

Heat potato slices and 3 cups water to boiling. Reduce heat; simmer until tender, 15 to 20 minutes. Rinse with cold water; drain. Place in large bowl; cover and chill.

In saucepan, blend sauce mix and oil; stir in ⅔ cup water and the vinegar. Heat to boiling over medium heat, stirring constantly. Cover and chill.

Blend mayonnaise and mustard: mix with potatoes, celery, onion, eggs and parsley.

6 servings.

SWEET POTATO CASSEROLE

1 can (18 ounces) vacuum-pack
  sweet potatoes
1 can (8¼ ounces) crushed pineapple
¼ cup chopped dates (sugar rolled)
1 tablespoon brown sugar
1 tablespoon butter or margarine
1 teaspoon salt
½ teaspoon nutmeg
1 cup miniature marshmallows

Heat oven to 350°. In ungreased 1½-quart casserole, mash sweet potatoes. Stir in remaining ingredients except ½ cup of the marshmallows; sprinkle with remaining marshmallows. Bake uncovered 30 minutes or until marshmallows are puffed and golden brown.

4 servings.

Substitution

For miniature marshmallows: 10 or 11 large marshmallows, cut up.

CARAMEL-GLAZED SWEET POTATOES

The skillet variation is pictured with the ham on page 5.

1 can (18 ounces) vacuum-pack
  sweet potatoes
½ teaspoon salt
⅓ cup caramel ice-cream topping

Heat oven to 350°. Arrange sweet potatoes in ungreased baking dish, 8 × 8 × 2 inches; season with salt. Spoon caramel topping on potatoes. Bake uncovered 25 to 30 minutes, basting occasionally with caramel topping in pan.

4 servings.

VARIATIONS

■ *Skillet-glazed Sweet Potatoes:* Arrange sweet potatoes in medium skillet; season with salt. Spoon ice-cream topping on potatoes. Heat just to boiling, stirring occasionally and carefully. (Don't cut or mash potatoes.) Reduce heat. Cook about 10 minutes longer, basting occasionally, until potatoes are heated through.

■ *Sweet Potatoes Orangé:* Substitute ⅓ cup orange marmalade for the caramel ice-cream topping.

Dinner Breads

SESAME RYE FINGERS

Pictured at right.

Spread 4 to 6 slices of rye bread with soft butter or margarine and sprinkle with sesame seed. Cut each slice crosswise into 4 strips; arrange on ungreased baking sheet. Set oven control at broil and/or 550°. Broil 6 inches from heat 1½ to 2 minutes or until seeds are brown.

4 to 6 servings.

BUN STICKS

Heat oven to 425°. Cut split halves of 3 or 4 frankfurter buns into 1-inch strips. Spread both sides of each strip with soft butter or margarine; arrange on ungreased baking sheet. Bake 5 to 8 minutes or until light brown.

12 to 16 sticks.

GARLIC FRENCH BREAD STICKS

The Parmesan variation is pictured at right.

¾ cup butter or margarine, melted
⅛ teaspoon instant minced garlic
1 loaf French bread, 19 × 3 × 2¼ inches

Heat oven to 425°. Mix butter and garlic. Cut bread into 5 pieces, each about 4 inches long; then cut each piece lengthwise into 6 sticks. Brush cut sides with garlic butter; arrange in ungreased jelly roll pan. Bake 8 minutes or until golden.

30 sticks.

VARIATIONS

■ *Dill French Sticks:* Omit garlic; sprinkle buttered sticks with 1 teaspoon dill weed.

■ *Parmesan French Sticks:* Omit garlic; sprinkle buttered sticks with ¼ cup Parmesan cheese.

ENGLISH MUFFIN DINNER ROUNDS

Parmesan rounds are pictured at right.

½ cup soft butter or margarine
½ teaspoon garlic salt
6 English muffins, split
1 to 2 tablespoons grated Parmesan cheese
    or sesame, poppy, celery or caraway seed

Mix butter and garlic salt; spread on cut surfaces of muffins. Sprinkle each with ¼ to ½ teaspoon Parmesan cheese.

Set oven control at broil and/or 550°. Broil muffins 4 inches from heat 5 to 6 minutes or until golden brown.

12 rounds.

HERB-TOPPED ROLLS

Heat oven to 400°. Brush tops of brown and serve rolls with melted butter or margarine. Sprinkle lightly with one of the following: parsley flakes or snipped chives, dill weed, onion salt or garlic salt, or a mixture of 1 teaspoon each tarragon leaves, sweet basil leaves and thyme leaves and ½ teaspoon ground sage. Bake 10 to 12 minutes or until golden brown.

CHEESE PUFFS

Pictured at right.

1 package brown and serve rolls
    (about 10 medium)
2 cups shredded cheese (8 ounces)
2 tablespoons soft butter or margarine
½ teaspoon dry mustard
½ teaspoon salt
⅛ teaspoon pepper

Slice rolls lengthwise in half. Mix remaining ingredients. Place about 1 tablespoon cheese mixture on each half; arrange on baking sheet. Bake as directed on package.

20 puffs.

Pictured at right:
From top to bottom—Sesame Rye Fingers,
English Muffin Dinner Rounds, Almond Flatbread,
Corn Sticks, Cheese Puffs, Parmesan French Sticks

RICH DINNER BISCUITS

Heat oven to 450°. Mix 2 cups buttermilk baking mix and ⅔ cup light cream (20%) until soft dough forms. Gently smooth dough into a ball on floured cloth-covered board. Knead 5 times; roll ½ inch thick. Cut with floured 2-inch cutter. Bake on ungreased baking sheet 8 to 10 minutes.

10 to 12 biscuits.

Substitution

For light cream: ½ cup milk and ¼ cup soft butter.

CHIVE DINNER MUFFINS

    2 cups buttermilk baking mix
    2 tablespoons shortening
    1 egg
    ⅔ cup milk or water
    ¼ cup snipped chives

Heat oven to 400°. Grease 12 medium muffin cups (2¾ inches in diameter). Mix all ingredients with fork; beat vigorously ½ minute. Fill muffin cups ⅔ full. Bake 15 minutes.

12 muffins.

BISCUIT FAN-TANS

    2 cups buttermilk baking mix
    ½ cup cold water
    ¼ cup butter or margarine, softened

Heat oven to 450°. Mix baking mix and water with fork until a soft dough forms. Gently smooth dough into a ball on floured cloth-covered board. Knead 5 times. Roll dough ¼ inch thick.

Spread half the butter on half of dough; fold over. Spread remaining butter on half of dough; fold in half again. Roll dough ½ inch thick. Cut with floured 2-inch cutter. Place 2 biscuits on sides in each ungreased muffin cup. Bake about 10 minutes.

8 or 9 fan-tans.

VARIATION

■ *Bacon Fan-tans:* Stir ¼ cup crumbled crisply fried bacon into the dough.

TWIN PAN ROLLS

Pictured on page 51.

    2 loaves frozen bread dough
    ½ teaspoon dill weed
    ½ teaspoon salt
    2 tablespoons butter or margarine, melted
    1 tablespoon parsley flakes
    2 tablespoons butter or margarine, melted
       About ½ cup shredded Parmesan
       cheese

Let bread dough thaw and rise as directed on package except—grease 2 layer pans, 8 or 9 × 1½ inches. Shape each loaf into 18 equal balls. Arrange 18 balls in one pan.

Mix dill weed, salt and 2 tablespoons butter. Brush dill mixture on rolls in pan; sprinkle with parsley flakes. Dip remaining rolls into 2 tablespoons butter, then dip tops in cheese and arrange in other pan. Cover; let rise 20 minutes.

Heat oven to 375°. Bake 15 minutes or until golden.

3 dozen rolls.

CORN POCKET ROLLS

    1½ cups all-purpose flour
    ½   cup cornmeal
    3   teaspoons baking powder
    ½   teaspoon salt
    2   tablespoons sugar
    1   egg, beaten
    ¾   cup dairy sour cream
    1   tablespoon soft butter or margarine

Heat oven to 375°. Mix flour, cornmeal, baking powder, salt and sugar. Mix egg and sour cream; stir into flour mixture. Roll dough ⅜ inch thick on floured board; cut into 3-inch rounds. Brush rounds with butter; fold in half. Press along folded edges. Bake on ungreased baking sheet 12 to 15 minutes.

10 rolls.

ALMOND FLATBREAD

Pictured on page 69.

- ¾ cup toasted almonds
- 1 cup all-purpose flour*
- 1½ teaspoons sugar
- ½ teaspoon salt
- ¼ teaspoon soda
- 2 tablespoons butter or margarine, softened
- ¼ cup dairy sour cream
- 3 tablespoons milk

Heat oven to 400°. Grind nuts in blender, watching carefully. (Or nuts can be finely chopped by hand.) Mix all ingredients with fork. Pinch off 1-inch balls. Roll each ball into 4-inch circle on floured board. Bake on ungreased baking sheet 6 to 8 minutes or until golden brown.

About 2½ dozen rounds.

*Do not use self-rising flour in this recipe.

PARMESAN SUPPER BREAD

- 1½ cups buttermilk baking mix
- 1 tablespoon sugar
- 1 tablespoon instant minced onion
- 1 egg
- ¼ cup milk
- ¼ cup white wine
- ½ teaspoon oregano
- ¼ cup grated Parmesan cheese

Heat oven to 400°. Grease layer pan, 8 × 1½ inches. Mix all ingredients except cheese with fork until a soft dough forms. Spread in pan; sprinkle with cheese. Bake 20 to 25 minutes. Cut into wedges.

6 to 8 servings.

Substitutions

For instant onion: 3 tablespoons finely chopped onion.

For wine: ¼ cup apple juice.

BREAD IN THE ROUND

- 4 cups buttermilk baking mix
- 1 package (1½ ounces) sour cream sauce mix
- 1¾ cups milk
- 2 eggs
  Poppy seed

Heat oven to 400°. Grease six 10-ounce custard cups. Mix all ingredients except poppy seed with fork until a soft dough forms; beat vigorously ½ minute. Spread in cups; sprinkle with poppy seed. Bake about 20 minutes.

6 rounds.

BISCUIT QUICK BREAD

Heat oven to 450°. Prepare Biscuit dough (enough for 10 to 12 biscuits) as directed on buttermilk baking mix package except—do not knead. Spread or roll dough on greased baking sheet into a rectangle, 10 × 8 inches. Spread dough with 1 tablespoon soft butter or margarine. Bake 10 minutes. Serve hot, broken into pieces or cut into squares.

6 servings.

VARIATION

■ *Caraway Quick Bread:* Stir 1 teaspoon caraway seed into dough. Sprinkle salt and paprika on buttered dough.

CORN BREAD

Corn Sticks are pictured on page 69.

- 2 eggs
- 1 cup buttermilk baking mix
- 1 cup white or yellow cornmeal
- 1½ cups buttermilk
- 2 tablespoons salad oil

Heat oven to 450°. Grease generously 12 medium muffin cups (2¾ inches in diameter), corn stick pans or baking pan, 9 × 9 × 2 inches. Heat in oven. Beat eggs with rotary beater until fluffy. Beat in remaining ingredients *just* until smooth. (Do not overbeat corn bread batter.)

Pour or spoon batter into hot pans until almost full. Bake muffins or corn sticks 15 to 20 minutes; corn bread 20 to 25 minutes. Serve piping hot.

12 servings.

Pasta and Rice

NOODLE STIR-INS

Cook 8 ounces egg noodles as directed on package. Just before serving, try your choice of the following additions:

■ *Almonds:* Brown ¼ cup sliced almonds in 2 tablespoons melted butter; stir into noodles.

■ *Browned Crumbs:* Brown ½ cup fine bread crumbs in 2 tablespoons melted butter; stir into noodles.

■ *Herbs:* Stir ½ teaspoon each thyme leaves, basil leaves, snipped parsley and chopped chives or minced onion into 2 tablespoons melted butter; stir into noodles.

■ *Onion and Green Pepper:* Cook and stir ¼ cup chopped green pepper and 2 tablespoons chopped onion in 2 tablespoons melted butter until onion is tender; stir into noodles.

■ *Parmesan:* Stir in 2 tablespoons melted butter, then fold in ¼ cup grated Parmesan cheese.

■ *Poppy Seed:* Stir in 2 teaspoons poppy seed and 1 tablespoon soft butter.

BACON AND ONION NOODLES

  3 **teaspoons salt**
  5 **ounces uncooked noodles (about 3 cups)**
  4 **slices bacon**
  1 **small onion, chopped**

Heat 6 cups water and the salt to boiling. Add noodles; heat to boiling. Boil uncovered, stirring occasionally, 7 to 10 minutes or until tender; drain.

While noodles cook, fry bacon until crisp; remove bacon and drain. Drain off all but 2 tablespoons fat. Cook and stir onion in fat until tender. Toss hot noodles with chopped onion and fat; crumble bacon on noodles.

4 to 6 servings.

CAULIFLOWER AND SPINACH NOODLES

  1 **small cauliflower (about 1 pound)**
  3 **teaspoons salt**
  5 **ounces uncooked spinach noodles (about 3 cups)**
  1 **package (about 1½ ounces) hollandaise sauce mix**
     Pimiento strips

Heat 1 inch salted water (½ teaspoon salt to 1 cup water) to boiling; add cauliflower. Cover tightly; heat to boiling. Reduce heat. Cook 15 to 20 minutes or until tender; drain.

While cauliflower cooks, heat 6 cups water and the 3 teaspoons salt to boiling. Add noodles; heat to boiling. Boil uncovered, stirring occasionally, 7 to 10 minutes or until tender; drain.

Prepare hollandaise sauce as directed on package. Turn noodles onto platter; arrange cauliflower in center of noodles. Pour sauce on cauliflower and garnish with pimiento.

4 servings.

ITALIAN RICE AND SPAGHETTI

  1 **cup boiling water**
  1 **cup tomato juice**
  ½ **envelope (2-ounce size) spaghetti sauce mix (about 2 tablespoons)**
     About 2 ounces uncooked long spaghetti, broken into 3-inch lengths
  ⅓ **cup uncooked converted rice**
  ½ **cup thinly sliced celery**

Heat oven to 350°. Heat water, tomato juice and spaghetti sauce mix to boiling, stirring occasionally. Mix all ingredients in ungreased 1½-quart casserole.

Cover tightly; bake 35 to 40 minutes, stirring after 20 minutes of baking. Uncover; bake 5 minutes longer or until rice and spaghetti are tender.

5 servings.

SAUCY SPAGHETTI AND SPROUTS

Pictured on page 51.

- 1 package (10 ounces) frozen
  Brussels sprouts
- 1 can (11 ounces) condensed Cheddar
  cheese soup
- ⅓ cup milk
- 3 teaspoons salt
  About 3½ ounces uncooked long spaghetti

Cook Brussels sprouts as directed on package ex-cept—decrease cooking time by 5 minutes; drain. Mix cheese soup and milk in saucepan. Return sprouts to saucepan. Cook over medium heat, stir-ring occasionally, 5 minutes or until sauce is heated through.

While Brussels sprouts cook, heat 6 cups water and the salt to boiling. Add spaghetti; heat to boiling. Boil uncovered, stirring occasionally, 7 to 10 min-utes or until tender; drain. Turn spaghetti onto platter; top with Brussels sprouts and sauce.

4 or 5 servings.

TOMATOED MACARONI

- 1 can (16 ounces) tomatoes
- 2 tablespoons butter or margarine
- 1 teaspoon salt
- ¼ teaspoon oregano
- 3 teaspoons salt
- 2 cups uncooked elbow macaroni
  Grated Parmesan cheese

Heat tomatoes, butter, 1 teaspoon salt and the oregano to boiling. Reduce heat; simmer 10 to 12 minutes, stirring occasionally.

While tomato sauce cooks, heat 6 cups water and the 3 teaspoons salt to boiling. Add macaroni; heat to boiling. Boil uncovered, stirring occasionally, 7 to 10 minutes or until tender; drain. Turn macaroni into serving dish; pour sauce on macaroni and sprin-kle with cheese.

6 servings.

OVEN STEAMED RICE

- 1 cup uncooked regular rice
- 2 cups boiling water
- 1 teaspoon salt

Heat oven to 350°. Mix all ingredients in ungreased 1- or 1½-quart casserole or in baking dish, 10 × 6 × 1½ or 11½ × 7½ × 1½ inches. Cover tightly; bake until liquid is absorbed and rice is tender, 25 to 30 minutes.

4 to 6 servings.

VARIATIONS

■ *Coconut Rice:* Decrease water to 1 cup and heat 1 cup milk and the water to boiling. Stir in ½ cup flaked coconut and 1 medium onion, thinly sliced.

■ *Mushroom-Herb Rice:* Increase salt to 1½ tea-spoons; stir in 1 can (4 ounces) mushroom stems and pieces, drained, 1 tablespoon instant chicken bouillon, 1 medium onion, thinly sliced, 1 table-spoon butter or margarine and ½ to 1 teaspoon chervil or 1 teaspoon parsley flakes.

■ *Orange Rice:* Decrease water to 1⅓ cups and heat ⅔ cup orange juice and the water to boiling. Stir in ¼ teaspoon allspice.

SKILLET PILAF

- 3 tablespoons butter or margarine
  Uncooked instant or converted rice
  (enough for 6 servings)
- 1 small onion, chopped
- 2 teaspoons instant beef bouillon
- ½ teaspoon salt
- ½ teaspoon ground cardamom
- ¼ teaspoon turmeric
- ¼ teaspoon allspice
- ⅛ teaspoon pepper

Melt butter in large skillet; cook and stir rice in butter until brown. Remove from heat. Stir in amount of water as directed on package for 6 serv-ings and the remaining ingredients. Cook as di-rected on package or until liquid is absorbed and rice is tender.

6 servings.

RICE MEDLEY

Pictured on page 51.

- 1 can (17 ounces) peas and tiny onions, drained (reserve liquid)
- 1½ cups uncooked instant rice
- 1 teaspoon butter or margarine
- ½ teaspoon salt
- 1 small carrot, shredded (about 3 tablespoons)

Add enough water to reserved liquid to measure 1½ cups; pour into 2-quart saucepan. Heat to boiling. Stir in peas, rice, butter, salt and shredded carrot; heat to boiling. Remove from heat. Cover tightly; let stand until liquid is absorbed and rice is tender, about 10 minutes.

4 to 6 servings.

CURRIED RICE

- Uncooked instant or converted rice (enough for 6 servings)
- 1 tablespoon instant minced onion
- 2 teaspoons instant chicken bouillon
- 1 teaspoon curry powder
- ¼ teaspoon pepper
- ⅛ teaspoon instant minced garlic

Cook rice as directed on package except—decrease salt to ½ teaspoon and stir in remaining ingredients with the water. Cook until liquid is absorbed and rice is tender.

6 servings.

HOPPING JOHN

- 1 package (10 ounces) frozen blackeye peas
- 4 slices bacon, diced
- 2 cups water
- 1½ teaspoons salt
- ½ cup uncooked converted rice

In covered saucepan, heat all ingredients except rice to boiling. Reduce heat; cook 20 minutes. Stir in rice; cook 25 minutes longer or until liquid is absorbed and rice is tender.

4 or 5 servings.

CARIBBEAN RICE AND BEANS

- Uncooked instant rice (enough for 4 servings)
- 1 can (15½ ounces) kidney beans, drained
- ½ teaspoon salt
- ⅛ teaspoon pepper
- ⅛ teaspoon instant minced garlic
- 2 tablespoons salad oil
- 1 tablespoon snipped chives

Cook rice as directed on package. While rice cooks, cook and stir beans, salt, pepper and garlic in oil until beans are heated through. Stir chives into rice. Turn rice onto platter; top with beans.

4 servings.

Substitution

For instant garlic: 1 clove garlic, minced.

Pictured at right:

TOP
Mocha Brownies/Chocolate Chip Bars
Fruit and Cheese Tray
Apple Pandowdy

CENTER
Broiled Fruit Kabobs
Cotton Candy Angel Cake
Cherry Cobbler

BOTTOM
Rocky Road Pudding
Orange Frost Soda
Double Fudge Cake

Desserts and Snacks

Strawberry Chantilly Torte

Butterscotch Crunch Cake

Cakes

STRAWBERRY CHANTILLY TORTE
1 package (18.5 ounces) white cake mix
  with pudding
1 package (15.4 ounces) creamy white
  frosting mix
1 package (8 ounces) cream cheese,
  softened
1 tablespoon milk
1 teaspoon almond extract
1 pint strawberries

Bake cake in 2 layer pans, 8 or 9 × 1½ inches, as directed on package. Cool; split to make 4 layers.

In small mixer bowl, beat frosting mix (dry), cream cheese, milk and almond extract until smooth. Slice strawberries lengthwise, reserving ½ cup of the outer slices for top layer.

Stack layers, spreading each with about ½ cup frosting and about ½ cup strawberries. Place reserved strawberry slices cut side down on top layer. Chill at least 1 hour before serving. Because of the cream cheese, refrigerate leftover cake.

LEMONADE CAKE
1 package (18.5 ounces) yellow cake mix
  with pudding
1 can (6 ounces) frozen lemonade concentrate,
  thawed
¾ cup confectioners' sugar

Heat oven to 350°. Grease and flour baking pan, 13 × 9 × 2 inches. Prepare cake mix as directed on package except—add enough water to ⅓ cup of the lemonade concentrate to measure 1 cup.

Pour into pan. Bake 35 to 40 minutes or until top springs back when touched lightly in center. Cool about 15 minutes. Mix remaining concentrate and the sugar. Prick warm cake with fork; drizzle concentrate mixture carefully over cake. Serve warm or cool. If desired, serve with whipped cream.

BUTTERSCOTCH CRUNCH CAKE

1 package (18.5 ounces) yellow cake mix
  with pudding
2 cans (5 ounces each) butterscotch pudding
1 cup crushed peanut brittle

Bake cake in baking pan, 13×9×2 inches, as directed on package. Cool; spread pudding on cake. Sprinkle with peanut brittle.

DOUBLE FUDGE CAKE

Pictured on page 75.

1 package (18.5 ounces) devils food cake
  mix with pudding
2 packages (6 ounces each) semisweet
  chocolate pieces
½ cup coarsely chopped nuts

Bake cake in baking pan, 13×9×2 inches, as directed on package. Sprinkle hot cake with chocolate pieces; cover with baking sheet. Let stand 3 to 5 minutes or until chocolate pieces are soft. Spread chocolate to frost cake. Sprinkle with nuts.

PARTY DEVILS FOOD CAKE

1 package (18.5 ounces) devils food
  cake mix with pudding
1 package (7.2 ounces) fluffy white
  frosting mix
8 maraschino cherries, chopped
1 can (4 ounces) shredded coconut
½ teaspoon almond extract

Bake cake in 2 layer pans, 8 or 9×1½ inches, as directed on package. Cool.

Prepare frosting as directed on package except—fold in almond extract; frost cake. Mix cherries and coconut until coconut is a delicate pink. Sprinkle on frosted cake.

Starting with a mix...
POUND CAKE VARIATIONS

Prepare 1 package (16 ounces) golden pound cake mix as directed except—try one of the following variations:

■ *Chocolate-Nut:* Stir in 2 squares (1 ounce each) unsweetened chocolate, grated, and ½ cup nuts.

■ *Fruit-Nut:* Stir in ½ cup finely chopped mixed candied fruit and ½ cup finely chopped nuts.

■ *Lemon:* Stir in 1 tablespoon grated lemon peel.

■ *Pecan:* Stir in 1 cup finely chopped pecans.

■ *Raisin-Nut:* Stir in ½ cup finely chopped raisins and ½ cup chopped nuts.

APPLESAUCE BUNDT CAKE

Heat oven to 350°. Generously grease 6-cup bundt cake pan. Prepare 1 package (15 ounces) applesauce raisin cake mix as directed except—mix in bowl.

Pour into pan. Bake 33 to 38 minutes or until top springs back when touched lightly in center. Cool 10 minutes; remove from pan. Cool completely. Spread top with Orange Glaze (below), allowing some to drizzle unevenly down side.

ORANGE GLAZE

Mix 1 cup confectioners' sugar, ½ teaspoon grated orange peel and 1 to 2 tablespoons orange juice until glaze is of proper consistency.

QUICK DATE CAKE

1 package (14 ounces) date bar mix
½ cup hot water
2 eggs
1 teaspoon baking powder
½ cup chopped walnuts

Heat oven to 375°. Grease baking pan, 8×8×2 inches. Mix date filling and hot water. Stir in crumbly mix, eggs, baking powder and nuts. Spread in pan. Bake about 30 minutes or until top springs back when touched lightly with finger. Cool.

Note: Recipe can be doubled and baked in greased baking pan, 13×9×2 inches.

ROOT BEER ANGEL CAKE

The Cotton Candy variation is pictured on page 75.

Prepare 1 package (15 or 16 ounces) angel food cake mix as directed except—substitute root beer flavored carbonated beverage for the water. Cool. Pour or spoon small amount of Root Beer Glaze (below) at a time on cake and spread, allowing some to drizzle unevenly down side.

ROOT BEER GLAZE

Melt ⅓ cup butter or margarine in saucepan. Remove from heat. Blend in 2 cups confectioners' sugar and ¼ cup finely crushed root beer-flavored hard candies. Stir in 2 to 4 tablespoons root beer-flavored carbonated beverage, 1 tablespoon at a time, until glaze is of proper consistency.

VARIATION

■ *Cotton Candy Angel Cake:* Substitute strawberry-flavored soda for the root beer-flavored carbonated beverage. In the glaze, omit crushed hard candies and use water or strawberry-flavored soda.

MOCK PISTACHIO CAKE

½ cup diced almonds
4 or 5 drops green food color
1 package (15 or 16 ounces) angel food
   cake mix
   Glaze (below)

Heat oven to 375°. In plastic bag or tightly covered jar, shake almonds and food color until almonds are evenly colored. Spread in ungreased baking pan. Bake 8 to 10 minutes. Cool.

Prepare cake as directed on package except—fold almonds into batter. Cool.

Pour or spoon small amount of Glaze at a time on top of cake and spread, allowing some to drizzle unevenly down side. (Glaze will set within ½ hour.)

GLAZE

Mix 1½ cups confectioners' sugar and 1 to 2 tablespoons water until smooth.

VARIATION

■ *Chocolate Chip Angel Cake:* Omit almonds and green food color. Fold in ½ cup chocolate shot.

GRAHAM CRACKER TORTE

⅔ cup walnuts
1¼ cups graham cracker crumbs
1 tablespoon plus 1 teaspoon flour
1½ teaspoons baking powder
2 eggs
⅓ cup butter or margarine, softened
⅔ cup sugar
½ cup milk
1 can (17.5 ounces) chocolate pudding
   Dessert topping or whipped cream
   Chopped crystallized ginger

Heat oven to 350°. Grease and flour layer pan, 9 × 1½ inches. Chop nuts 10 seconds in blender. Mix nuts, crumbs, flour and baking powder in bowl.

In blender, whip eggs, butter and sugar ½ minute while adding milk. Whip 1 minute longer, adding crumb mixture and stopping blender occasionally to scrape sides and guide mixture toward blades.

Pour batter into pan. Bake 40 minutes. Cool 10 minutes in pan; remove and cool. Split to make 2 layers. Fill layers and frost top with pudding. Garnish with dessert topping and ginger. Because of the pudding, refrigerate leftover torte.

8 to 10 servings.

Substitution

For chocolate pudding: 1 can (17.5 ounces) vanilla pudding or 2 cups sweetened whipped cream.

Note: To make graham cracker crumbs in blender, use 18 to 20 graham crackers. Break 5 or 6 crackers at a time into blender; grind 10 seconds and empty into measuring cup. Repeat until crumbs measure 1¼ cups.

The Cake Pan Counts—a Lot

Obvious but important, use the right size pan. Shiny metal ones give you tender, light brown crusts. (With heat-resistant glass pans, just lower the oven temperature 25°.) Nonstick finishes are great, too. Simply do as the manufacturer says.

For layer or loaf cakes (mix or scratch), grease pans generously with shortening—not butter, margarine or oil. Dust with abandon, shaking out the excess flour. Place pans on the middle rack of the oven and don't let them touch—the sides or each other.

BLENDER ORANGE-RAISIN CAKE

    1   orange
    1   egg
    ⅓   cup shortening
    ¾   cup milk
    1   teaspoon vanilla
    1¼ cups all-purpose flour*
    1   cup sugar
    1½ teaspoons baking powder
    ½   teaspoon salt
    ½   cup walnuts
    ½   cup raisins
        Creamy Orange Frosting (below)

Heat oven to 350°. Grease and flour baking pan, 9×9×2 or 8×8×2 inches. With vegetable parer, remove thin outer layer of peel from orange. (Set orange aside and use for juice in frosting.) Place peel in blender; chop on low speed and set chopped peel aside.

In order listed, measure egg, shortening, milk, vanilla, flour, sugar, baking powder, salt, walnuts and raisins into blender; add 1 tablespoon of the chopped peel (reserve ½ teaspoon chopped peel for frosting). Mix ½ minute on high speed, stopping blender occasionally to scrape sides with rubber spatula. (Batter may be slightly lumpy.)

Pour batter into pan. Bake 9-inch square about 35 minutes, 8-inch square about 40 minutes or until wooden pick inserted in center comes out clean. Cool; frost with Creamy Orange Frosting.

*If using self-rising flour, omit baking powder and salt.

Note: To prepare cake with electric mixer, measure all ingredients except orange and frosting into large mixer bowl, using 1 teaspoon grated orange peel, ½ cup chopped walnuts and ½ cup chopped raisins. Blend ½ minute on low speed, scraping bowl constantly. Beat 3 minutes high speed, scraping bowl occasionally.

CREAMY ORANGE FROSTING

    ⅓   cup butter or margarine, softened
    1½ teaspoons vanilla
    2   tablespoons orange juice
    ½   teaspoon reserved chopped orange peel
    2   cups confectioners' sugar

Mix all ingredients until smooth.

SPICE CAKE

    1¼ cups all-purpose flour*
    1   cup sugar
    1½ teaspoons baking powder
    1   teaspoon cinnamon
    ½   teaspoon salt
    ½   teaspoon nutmeg
    ¼   teaspoon cloves
    ¾   cup milk
    ⅓   cup shortening
    1   egg
        Browned Butter Icing (below)

Heat oven to 350°. Grease and flour baking pan, 8×8×2 or 9×9×2 inches. Measure all ingredients except Browned Butter Icing into large mixer bowl. Blend ½ minute on low speed, scraping bowl constantly. Beat 3 minutes high speed, scraping bowl occasionally.

Pour into pan. Bake 35 to 40 minutes or until wooden pick inserted in center comes out clean. Cool; frost with Browned Butter Icing.

*If using self-rising flour, omit baking powder and salt.

BROWNED BUTTER ICING

    3   tablespoons butter or margarine
    1½ cups confectioners' sugar
    1   teaspoon vanilla
        About 1 tablespoon milk

Heat butter in saucepan over medium heat until a delicate brown. Blend in sugar. Stir in vanilla and milk; beat until frosting is smooth and of spreading consistency.

Substitution

For all-purpose flour: 1½ cups cake flour.

Hideaways for Frosted Cakes

With a creamy-type frosting: Keep under a cake safe or an inverted large bowl. Or cover loosely with foil, plastic wrap or waxed paper.

With a fluffy-type frosting: Eat right away! If you must store, or have some left over, use a cake safe. But keep a knife under the edge to let a bit of air in.

With a whipped cream-type frosting: Store in the refrigerator—no need to cover. Do the same for any cake with a cream filling or topping.

Starting with a mix...
CHOCOLATE FROSTING VARIATIONS

Prepare 1 package (15.4 ounces) chocolate fudge frosting mix as directed except—try one of the following variations:

■ *Mocha:* Add 1 tablespoon powdered instant coffee.

■ *Peppermint:* Sprinkle top of frosted cake with ½ cup crushed peppermint candy.

■ *Peppermint Fudge:* Stir in ¼ to ½ teaspoon peppermint extract.

■ *Rocky Road:* Stir in ½ cup miniature marshmallows and ½ cup chopped nuts.

Starting with a mix...
CREAMY WHITE FROSTING VARIATIONS

Prepare 1 package (15.4 ounces) creamy white frosting mix as directed except—try one of the following variations:

■ *Browned Butter:* Lightly brown butter over low heat.

■ *Chocolate:* Add ½ cup cocoa.

■ *Cocoa Mocha:* Substitute strong coffee for the water and add ½ cup cocoa.

■ *Lemon, Orange or Lime:* Substitute lemon, orange or lime juice for the water.

■ *Peppermint:* Add ½ teaspoon peppermint extract and 3 to 4 drops food color.

■ *Raisin-Nut:* Stir in ½ cup cut-up raisins and ½ cup finely chopped nuts.

■ *Raspberry or Strawberry:* Substitute crushed fresh or thawed frozen raspberries or strawberries for the water.

Pictured at left:
Chocolate cake with Chocolate Chip Fluffy White
Frosting—a double dose of chocolate

Starting with a mix...
FLUFFY WHITE FROSTING VARIATIONS

Prepare 1 package (7.2 ounces) fluffy white frosting mix as directed except—try one of the following variations:

■ *Almond:* Fold in ½ teaspoon almond extract.

■ *Cherry-Nut:* Fold in ⅓ cup drained chopped maraschino cherries and ½ cup chopped nuts.

■ *Chocolate Chip:* Fold in ½ cup semisweet chocolate pieces.

■ *Cinnamon:* Add 1 teaspoon cinnamon.

■ *Clove:* Add ¼ teaspoon cloves.

■ *Lemon:* Fold in ½ teaspoon lemon extract.

■ *Maple-Nut:* Fold in ½ teaspoon maple flavoring and ½ cup chopped pecans.

■ *Mocha:* Add 2 teaspoons powdered instant coffee.

■ *Nutmeg:* Add ½ teaspoon nutmeg.

■ *Orange-Coconut:* Fold in 1 tablespoon grated orange peel and ½ cup finely cut-up coconut.

■ *Orange-Raisin:* Fold in ½ cup chopped nuts, 1½ cups raisins and 2 tablespoons coarsely grated orange peel.

■ *Peppermint:* Fold in ¼ teaspoon peppermint extract. Red or green food color can be added.

■ *Spice:* Add ½ teaspoon cinnamon, ¼ teaspoon nutmeg and ¼ teaspoon cloves.

Frosting a Layer Cake?

Is the cake nice and cool? Okay, begin. Lift one layer in your hand. With your free hand, brush the sides and edges gently to remove excess crumbs. Do the same with the other layer.

Place one layer upside down on the cake plate. Use about ½ cup frosting to fill—but don't spread to the edge; leave about ¼ inch free of filling. Then place the second layer right side up on the filling.

Now to the business of frosting. Do the sides first. Start with a thin coat to seal in the crumbs, then once again lavishly. Bring the frosting up high on the side, forming a ridge above the top. Spread the remaining frosting on top, meeting the ridge. It's picture pretty this way—don't you agree?

VANILLA BUTTER FROSTING

⅓ cup soft butter or margarine
3 cups confectioners' sugar
1½ teaspoons vanilla
   About 2 tablespoons milk

Blend butter and sugar. Stir in vanilla and milk; beat until frosting is smooth and of spreading consistency.

Fills and frosts two 8- or 9-inch layers or frosts a 13 × 9-inch cake.

VARIATIONS

■ *Browned Butter Frosting:* Heat butter in saucepan over medium heat until a delicate brown.

■ *Cherry Butter Frosting:* Stir in 2 tablespoons drained chopped maraschino cherries and 2 drops red food color.

■ *Orange Butter Frosting:* Omit vanilla and substitute orange juice for the milk; stir in 2 teaspoons grated orange peel.

■ *Peanut Butter Frosting:* Substitute peanut butter for the butter; increase milk to ¼ to ⅓ cup.

CHOCOLATE BUTTER FROSTING

⅓ cup soft butter or margarine
2 ounces melted unsweetened chocolate
   (cool)
2 cups confectioners' sugar
1½ teaspoons vanilla
   About 2 tablespoons milk

Mix thoroughly butter and cooled chocolate. Blend in sugar. Stir in vanilla and milk; beat until frosting is smooth and of spreading consistency.

Fills and frosts two 8- or 9-inch layers or frosts a 13 × 9-inch cake.

VARIATIONS

■ *Chocolate-Nut Butter Frosting:* Stir in ¼ cup finely chopped nuts.

■ *Cocoa Butter Frosting:* Substitute ⅓ cup cocoa for the chocolate.

■ *Mocha Butter Frosting:* Blend in 1½ teaspoons powdered instant coffee with the sugar.

CHOCOLATE GLAZE

In small bowl, blend ¼ cup canned chocolate frosting and 2 teaspoons hot water. If necessary, add a few drops of water until of desired consistency.

Glazes an 8- or 9-inch layer cake.

BUTTERSCOTCH BROILED TOPPING

¼ cup soft butter or margarine
⅔ cup brown sugar (packed)
1 cup finely chopped nuts
2 tablespoons milk

Mix thoroughly butter, brown sugar and nuts. Stir in milk. Spread mixture evenly on warm 13 × 9-inch cake.

Set oven control at broil and/or 550°. Place cake 5 inches from heat; broil about 3 minutes or until topping bubbles and browns slightly. (Watch carefully—mixture burns easily.)

Frosts a 13 × 9-inch cake.

VARIATIONS

■ *Coconut Broiled Topping:* Decrease nuts to ½ cup; add 1 cup flaked coconut with the nuts and increase milk to 3 tablespoons.

■ *Crunchy Broiled Topping:* Decrease nuts to ½ cup; add ½ cup whole wheat flake cereal with the nuts and increase milk to 3 tablespoons.

BROWN SUGAR MERINGUE

2 egg whites (¼ cup)
1 cup brown sugar (packed)
1 tablespoon lemon juice
½ cup finely chopped nuts

Just before cake is removed from oven, beat egg whites until foamy. Gradually beat sugar and lemon juice into egg whites, beating until stiff. Carefully spread on hot 13 × 9-inch cake. Sprinkle with nuts. Bake in 400° oven 8 to 10 minutes or until brown.

Frosts a 13 × 9-inch cake.

Pies

APPLE-CHEESE PIE

    Pastry for 9-inch Two-crust Pie (page 87)
1   cup shredded Cheddar cheese (4 ounces)
2   cans (21 ounces each) apple pie filling

Heat oven to 425°. Prepare pastry except—add cheese before mixing. Fill pastry-lined pie pan with apple pie filling.

Cover with top crust which has slits cut in it; seal and flute. Cover edge with 2- to 3-inch strip of aluminum foil to prevent excessive browning; remove foil for the last 15 minutes of baking. Bake 35 to 40 minutes.

Starting with a frozen pie...
APPLE PIE FIX-UPS

Bake 8-inch frozen ready-to-bake apple pie as directed on package except—try one of the following variations:

■ *Cheesy Apple Pie:* Five minutes before end of baking time, spread ½ cup pasteurized process cheese spread on pie.

■ *Raspberry-glazed Apple Pie:* Five minutes before end of baking time, spread 2 tablespoons raspberry jam on pie.

■ *Vanilla Apple Pie:* After baking, pour 2 teaspoons vanilla into slits in crust. Best served warm.

■ *Orange-glazed Apple Pie:* Mix ½ cups confectioners' sugar, 2 teaspoons grated orange peel and 1 tablespoon orange juice. Spoon on warm baked pie; garnish with orange slices.

APPLE PANDOWDY

Pictured on page 75.

    Pastry for 8- or 9-inch Two-crust Pie
    (page 87)
1   can (20 ounces) apple slices,
    drained
½   cup brown sugar (packed)
3   tablespoons butter or margarine,
    melted
6   tablespoons maple-flavored syrup

Heat oven to 425°. Prepare pastry. Mix apple slices and brown sugar. Fill pastry-lined pie pan with apple mixture; top with butter and 3 tablespoons of the syrup.

Cover with top crust which has slits cut in it; seal and flute. Bake 15 minutes. Remove from oven; make crisscross cuts about 1 inch apart through top crust and apples. Pour remaining syrup on crust.

Cover edge with 2- to 3-inch strip of aluminum foil to prevent excessive browning. Bake 25 minutes. Serve warm and, if you like, with maple-flavored syrup.

VARIATION

■ *Molasses Pandowdy:* Substitute 3 tablespoons corn syrup for first 3 tablespoons maple-flavored syrup and 3 tablespoons molasses for the second.

RASPBERRY PIE

    Pastry for 9-inch Two-crust Pie (page 87)
¼   cup sugar
3   tablespoons flour
3   packages (10 ounces each) frozen
    raspberries, thawed and drained
    (reserve ½ cup syrup)
2   tablespoons butter or margarine

Heat oven to 425°. Prepare pastry. Combine sugar and flour; mix with raspberries and reserved syrup. Pour into pastry-lined pie pan; dot with butter.

Cover with top crust which has slits cut in it; seal and flute. Cover edge with 2- to 3-inch strip of aluminum foil to prevent excessive browning; remove foil for the last 15 minutes of baking. Bake 35 to 40 minutes.

BERRY BASKET PIE

  9-inch Cookie Pat Crust (page 87)
4 cups fresh strawberries (about 2 pints)
1 envelope (about 1½ ounces) whipped
  topping mix
1 can (17.5 ounces) vanilla pudding

Bake crust; cool. Reserve about 8 strawberries for garnish. Arrange remaining whole berries in baked crust. Prepare whipped topping as directed on package. Fold topping into pudding; pour on berries in crust. Chill at least 4 hours. Garnish with reserved berries. For easier cutting, let stand at room temperature 10 minutes before serving.

Substitution

  For Cookie Pat Crust: Vanilla Wafer Cookie Crumb Crust (page 87).

PERFECT PINEAPPLE PIE

  Pastry for 9-inch Two-crust Pie (page 87)
3 eggs
⅓ cup butter or margarine, melted
2 tablespoons lemon juice
½ cup water
1 cup sugar
¼ cup all-purpose flour*
¼ teaspoon salt
1 can (20 ounces) crushed pineapple,
  drained

Heat oven to 400°. Prepare pastry. In small mixer bowl, beat eggs until blended. Add butter, lemon juice and water; blend on low speed. Add sugar, flour and salt; beat until smooth. Stir in pineapple. Fill pastry-lined pie pan with pineapple mixture.

Cut second half of pastry into ten ½-inch strips. Arrange 5 pastry strips 1 inch apart across filling. Weave first cross-strip through center. Add another cross-strip, first folding back every other strip going the other way. Continue weaving until lattice is complete.

Fold lower crust over ends of pastry strips, building up edge; seal and flute. Cover edge with 2- to 3-inch strip of aluminum foil to prevent excessive browning; remove foil for the last 15 minutes of baking. Bake 35 to 40 minutes.

*If using self-rising flour, omit salt.

Starting with a frozen pie...
CHERRY PIE FIX-UPS

Bake 8-inch frozen ready-to-bake cherry pie as directed on package except—try one of the following variations:

■ *Candy-topped Cherry Pie:* Five minutes before end of baking time, sprinkle 1 bar (1⅛ ounces) chocolate toffee candy, chopped, on pie. After baking, pour 1 tablespoon crème de cacao or chocolate syrup into slits in crust.

■ *Lemon-glazed Cherry Pie:* Ten minutes before end of baking time, spread pie with Lemon Glaze: Mix ½ cup confectioners' sugar, 1 teaspoon grated lemon peel and 1 tablespoon lemon juice until smooth. (Be sure to drizzle some of the glaze into slits in crust.)

ORANGE-CHERRY PIE

  Pastry for 8-inch Two-crust Pie (page 87)
1 tablespoon finely shredded orange peel
1 can (21 ounces) cherry pie filling
½ cup confectioners' sugar
1 teaspooon shredded orange peel
1 tablespoon orange juice

Heat oven to 425°. Prepare pastry except—add 1 tablespoon orange peel. Mix remaining ingredients. Fill pastry-lined pie pan with cherry mixture.

Cut second half of pastry into eight ½-inch strips. Arrange 4 pastry strips 1 inch apart across filling. Weave first cross-strip, folding back every other strip going the other way. Continue weaving cross-strips in this manner until lattice is complete.

Fold lower crust over ends of pastry strips, building up edge; seal and flute. Cover edge with 2- to 3-inch strip of aluminum foil to prevent excessive browning; remove foil for the last 15 minutes of baking. Bake 35 to 40 minutes.

Pictured at right:
Orange-Cherry Pie

PECAN PIE

 3 **eggs**
⅔ **cup sugar**
½ **teaspoon salt**
⅓ **cup butter or margarine, melted**
 1 **cup light or dark corn syrup**
 1 **cup pecan halves or broken pieces**
   9-inch frozen ready-to-bake pie crust shell

Heat oven to 375°. Beat eggs, sugar, salt, butter and syrup with rotary beater. Stir in nuts. Pour into frozen pie crust shell. Bake 40 to 50 minutes or until filling is set.

Substitution

For ready-to-bake pie crust shell: Pastry for 9-inch One-crust Pie (page 87).

Starting with a frozen pie...
PUMPKIN PIE FIX-UPS

Bake 8-inch frozen ready-to-bake pumpkin pie as directed on package. Then try one of the following variations:

■ *Maple Pumpkin Pie:* Cool pie about 30 minutes. Drizzle 2 tablespoons maple-flavored syrup on warm pie; sprinkle with 2 tablespoons chopped pecans. Serve warm.

■ *Pumpkin Pie with Rum Whipped Topping:* Cool pie about 1 hour. Mix ½ carton (8-ounce size) whipped cream cheese, 2 tablespoons confectioners' sugar and 1 tablespoon rum or ½ teaspoon rum flavoring; spread topping on warm pie. Serve pie immediately.

Pastry a Problem?

It needn't be—if you follow directions carefully and add these tips to your repertoire:

Rolling out: Keep the pastry circle round by pushing in gently around the edge with slightly cupped hands.

Patching up: Moisten the edge or tear; press the pastry patch into place. Who can tell?

Transferring: Fold the pastry round in quarters, then place in the pie pan with the point at center; unfold. It's an easy job this way.

STRAWBERRY CREAM PIE

   9-inch Graham Cracker Crust (page 87)
 1 **package (10 ounces) frozen strawberries**
 1 **package (3 ounces) strawberry-flavored gelatin**
 1 **pint vanilla ice cream**

Bake crust; cool. Heat strawberries to boiling, breaking apart with fork. Stir in gelatin until dissolved. Mix in ice cream until melted. Chill until thickened but not set.

Pour into baked crust. Chill until firm, about 2 hours. If desired, serve wih frozen dessert topping (thawed) or sweetened whipped cream.

Substitution

For Graham Cracker Crust: 9-inch purchased graham cracker crust, baked.

GRASSHOPPER PIE

   Chocolate Wafer Cookie Crumb Crust (page 87)
 3 **cups miniature marshmallows**
 ½ **cup milk**
1½ **cups chilled whipping cream**
 ¼ **cup green crème de menthe**
 3 **tablespoons white crème de cacao**
   Few drops green food color

Bake crust; cool. Melt marshmallows in milk over low heat, stirring constantly. Chill until thickened.

In chilled bowl, beat cream until stiff. Stir marshmallow mixture to blend; stir in liqueurs and fold into cream. Fold in food color. Pour into baked crust. If desired, sprinkle grated semisweet chocolate on top. Chill at least 4 hours.

Substitution

For miniature marshmallows: 32 large marshmallows, cut up.

ELECTRIC MIXER PASTRY

8- OR 9-INCH ONE-CRUST PIE
1 cup all-purpose flour*
½ teaspoon salt
⅓ cup plus 1 tablespoon shortening
2 to 3 tablespoons cold water

8- OR 9-INCH TWO-CRUST PIE
2 cups all-purpose flour*
1 teaspoon salt
⅔ cup plus 2 tablespoons shortening
4 to 5 tablespoons cold water

Measure flour, salt and shortening into large mixer bowl; blend 1 minute on low speed, scraping bowl constantly. Add water; mix until all flour is moistened and dough begins to gather into beaters, about 10 seconds. (If using quick-mixing flour, dough will begin to gather into beater in about 1 minute.) Scrape bowl constantly.

Press dough firmly into a ball. Shape into flattened round on lightly floured cloth-covered board. (For Two-crust Pie, divide dough in half and shape into 2 flattened rounds.) With floured stockinet-covered rolling pin, roll dough 2 inches larger than inverted pie pan.

Fold pastry into quarters; transfer to pie pan, unfold and ease into pan.

For One-crust Pie: Trim overhanging edge of pastry 1 inch from rim of pan. Fold and roll pastry under, even with pan; flute. Fill and bake as directed in recipe.

For Baked Pie Shell: Prick bottom and side thoroughly with fork. Bake in 475° oven 8 to 10 minutes.

For Two-crust Pie: Pour desired filling into pastry-lined pie pan. Trim overhanging edge of pastry ½ inch from rim of pan. Roll second round of dough. Fold into quarters; cut slits so steam can escape. Place over filling and unfold. Trim overhanging edge of pastry 1 inch from rim of pan. Fold and roll top edge under lower edge, pressing pastry on rim of pan to seal; flute. Bake as directed in recipe.

*If using self-rising flour, omit salt. Pie crusts made with self-rising flour differ in flavor and texture from those made with plain flour.

GRAHAM CRACKER CRUST

1½ cups graham cracker crumbs
     (about 20 crackers)
  3 tablespoons sugar
  ⅓ cup butter or margarine, melted

Heat oven to 350°. Mix crumbs, sugar and butter. (If desired, reserve 2 to 3 tablespoons crumb mixture for a garnish.) Press mixture firmly and evenly against bottom and side of 9-inch pie pan. Bake 10 minutes. Cool.

COOKIE CRUMB CRUST

1½ cups cookie crumbs (vanilla or
     chocolate wafers or gingersnaps)
  2 tablespoons sugar
  ¼ cup butter or margarine, melted

Heat oven to 350°. Mix crumbs, sugar and butter. (If desired, reserve 2 to 3 tablespoons crumb mixture for a garnish.) Press mixture firmly and evenly against bottom and side of 9-inch pie pan. Bake 10 minutes. Cool.

COOKIE PAT CRUST

  1 cup all-purpose flour*
  ½ cup butter or margarine, softened
  ¼ cup finely chopped pecans
  ¼ cup confectioners' sugar

Heat oven to 400°. With hands, mix all ingredients to form a soft dough. Press firmly and evenly against bottom and side of 9-inch pie pan. (Do not press on rim.) Bake 12 to 15 minutes or until light brown. Cool.

*Self-rising flour can be used in this recipe. If using quick-mixing flour, add 1 tablespoon milk.

Pastry from a Package

Skip the preliminaries. Get right down to the pastry rolling with a never-fail pie crust mix—either pie crust sticks or free-flowing mix. And since a mix puts you a jump ahead, think about this: do two shells at one time—one for today's pie and one to freeze, baked or unbaked.

Cookies

Starting with a mix...
BROWNIE VARIATIONS

Mocha Brownies are pictured on page 75.

Prepare 1 package (15 ounces) fudge brownie mix as directed except—try one of the following variations:

■ *Almond:* Stir in ½ teaspoon almond extract.

■ *Cherry:* Stir in ¼ cup drained chopped maraschino cherries (about 16).

■ *Coconut:* Omit nuts; stir in 1 cup flaked coconut.

■ *Date:* Omit nuts; stir in 1 cup chopped dates. Coat baked squares with confectioners' sugar.

■ *Fruit:* Stir in ⅓ cup chopped candied fruit.

■ *Mint:* Immediately after removing brownies from oven, place 16 chocolate-covered mint patties (about 1½ inches in diameter) on top. Allow mints to soften; spread evenly.

■ *Mocha:* Add 1½ tablespoons powdered instant coffee.

■ *Peanut:* Stir in ½ cup chopped peanuts. Frost with a peanut butter icing.

■ *Peanut Butter:* Omit nuts; add 3 tablespoons chunky peanut butter.

The Case for Keeping Cookies

Soft cookies: Store in any container with a tight-fitting cover. To keep them soft, tuck in a fresh slice of bread or apple every couple of days.

Crisp cookies: Store in any container, but cover loosely. If they soften, recrisp by placing them in a 300° oven for 3 to 5 minutes. Crunch!

Freezing? Arrange baked cookies in a foil- or plastic wrap-lined box, separating the layers with foil or wrap. Or, store small batches in freezer bags, plastic wrap or foil. They'll keep for 9 to 12 months!

GINGERBREAD DROPS

Heat oven to 375°. Blend 1 package (14.5 ounces) gingerbread mix (dry) and ½ cup water. Drop by teaspoonfuls about 2 inches apart onto lightly greased baking sheet. Bake 10 to 12 minutes.

About 3 dozen cookies.

VARIATIONS

■ *Chocolate Chip Ginger Drops:* Stir in 1 package (6 ounces) semisweet chocolate pieces and ½ cup chopped nuts.

■ *Coconut Ginger Drops:* Stir in 1 cup shredded coconut.

■ *Date-Nut Ginger Drops:* Stir in ½ cup cut-up dates and ½ cup chopped nuts.

■ *Jeweled Ginger Drops:* Stir in ⅔ cup cut-up gumdrops and ½ cup chopped nuts.

■ *Mincemeat Ginger Drops:* Stir in 1 cup prepared mincemeat and ½ cup chopped nuts.

■ *Peanut Butter Ginger Drops:* Add ½ cup peanut butter.

■ *Peanut Ginger Drops:* Stir in 1 cup chopped roasted peanuts.

■ *Raisin-Nut Ginger Drops:* Stir in 1 cup raisins and ½ cup chopped nuts.

Starting with a mix...
DATE BAR VARIATIONS

Prepare 1 package (14 ounces) date bar mix as directed except—try one of the following variations:

■ *Almond:* Stir ¾ teaspoon almond extract into date filling.

■ *Apple:* Stir ½ cup finely chopped pared tart apples into date filling.

■ *Apricot:* Stir ½ cup finely cut dried apricots into date filling.

■ *Cherry:* Stir ¼ cup drained chopped maraschino cherries (about 16) into date filling.

■ *Raisin:* Stir ½ cup raisins into date filling.

■ *Walnut:* Stir ½ cup chopped walnuts into date filling.

REFRIGERATOR COOKIES

　1　**package (15.4 ounces) creamy white frosting mix**
　2　**cups all-purpose flour***
　1　**cup butter or margarine, softened**
　½　**cup chopped pecans**
1½　**tablespoons butter or margarine, softened**
　2　**tablespoons hot water**

Measure 1½ cups of the frosting mix (dry) into large bowl. With hands, mix in flour, 1 cup butter and the pecans. Divide dough in half; shape each half into roll, about 1½ inches in diameter and about 7½ inches long. Wrap; chill at least 4 hours.

Heat oven to 400°. Cut rolls into ⅛-inch slices. Place 1 inch apart on ungreased baking sheet. Bake 4 to 6 minutes. Cool slightly before removing from baking sheet.

Mix remaining frosting mix, 1½ tablespoons soft butter and the water until smooth. (Add 1 to 2 teaspoons water if necessary.) Frost cookies. (Enough frosting for about 4 dozen cookies.)

About 8 dozen cookies.

*Do not use self-rising flour in this recipe.

VARIATION

■ *Chocolate Refrigerator Cookies:* Substitute chocolate fudge frosting mix for the creamy white.

GOLDEN GOOD BARS

　2　**cups buttermilk baking mix**
1½　**cups brown sugar (packed)**
　3　**eggs**
　1　**teaspoon vanilla**
　1　**cup chopped nuts**
　½　**cup flaked coconut**

Heat oven to 350°. Grease and flour baking pan, 13 × 9 × 2 inches. In large bowl, mix all ingredients. Spread in pan. Bake about 35 minutes. Cool; cut into bars, 2 × 1 inch.

4½ dozen cookies.

ALMOND SHORTBREADS

　1　**packet free-flowing pie crust mix**
　1　**cup confectioners' sugar**
　½　**cup chopped blanched almonds**
　1　**teaspoon almond extract**

Heat oven to 350°. Prepare pastry for Two-crust Pie as directed on package except—before adding water to pie crust mix, mix in sugar, nuts and almond extract.

Roll dough ½ inch thick on lightly floured board. Cut into 1¼-inch diamonds. Place ½ inch apart on ungreased baking sheet. Bake about 15 minutes or until set. Immediately remove from baking sheet.

About 3 dozen cookies.

Substitution

For free-flowing mix: 2 sticks pie crust mix.

CANDY COOKIES

　2　**cups sugar**
　¼　**cup cocoa**
　½　**cup milk**
　½　**cup butter or margarine**
　½　**cup peanut butter**
　2　**cups quick-cooking oats**
　2　**teaspoons vanilla**
　½　**cup chopped nuts**

In large saucepan, heat sugar, cocoa, milk and butter, stirring occasionally, until mixture boils. Boil 1 minute. Remove from heat; stir in remaining ingredients.

Drop by teaspoonfuls onto waxed paper. (Cookies will spread very thin.) Let stand about 40 minutes or until firm. Store in covered container in refrigerator.

About 4 dozen cookies.

CHOCOLATE CHIP BARS

Pictured on page 75.

⅓ cup shortening
⅓ cup butter or margarine, softened
½ cup granulated sugar
½ cup brown sugar (packed)
 1 egg
 1 teaspoon vanilla
1½ cups all-purpose flour*
½ teaspoon soda
¾ teaspoon salt
½ cup chopped pecans
 1 package (6 ounces) semisweet
   chocolate pieces

Heat oven to 375°. Mix shortening, butter, sugars, egg and vanilla. Stir in remaining ingredients.

Spread in ungreased baking pan, 13 × 9 × 2 inches. Bake 20 to 25 minutes or until light brown. Cool; cut into bars, about 3 × 1 inch.

About 3 dozen cookies.

*If using self-rising flour, omit soda and salt.

APPLESAUCE BARS

 1 cup all-purpose flour*
⅔ cup brown sugar (packed)
 1 teaspoon soda
 1 teaspoon pumpkin pie spice
½ teaspoon salt
¼ cup shortening
 1 cup applesauce
 1 egg
½ cup raisins
   Browned Butter Icing (below)

Heat oven to 350°. Grease baking pan, 13 × 9 × 2 inches. Mix all ingredients except icing. Spread in pan. Bake about 25 minutes. Cool; frost with icing. Cut into bars, about 3 × 1 inch.

32 cookies.

*If using self-rising flour, decrease soda to ½ teaspoon and omit salt.

BROWNED BUTTER ICING

Heat 3 tablespoons butter over medium heat until golden. Remove from heat; blend in 1½ cups confectioners' sugar, 1 teaspoon vanilla and about 1 tablespoon milk. Beat until smooth.

COCONUT-TOFFEE BARS

¼ cup butter or margarine, softened
¼ cup shortening
½ cup brown sugar (packed)
 1 cup all-purpose flour*
   Almond-Coconut Topping (below)

Heat oven to 350°. Cream butter, shortening and sugar. Blend in flour. Press evenly in bottom of ungreased baking pan, 13 × 9 × 2 inches. Bake 10 minutes.

Spread Almond-Coconut Topping on baked layer. Bake 25 minutes longer or until topping is golden brown. Cool cookies slightly; cut into bars, about 3 × 1 inch.

32 cookies.

*If using self-rising flour, omit baking powder and salt from Almond-Coconut Topping.

ALMOND-COCONUT TOPPING

 2 eggs
 1 cup brown sugar (packed)
 1 teaspoon vanilla
 2 tablespoons flour
 1 teaspoon baking powder
½ teaspoon salt
 1 cup shredded coconut
 1 cup chopped almonds

Beat eggs in large mixing bowl; stir in remaining ingredients.

PEANUT BREAK

 1 cup butter or margarine, melted
1½ cups brown sugar (packed)
 2 cups all-purpose flour*
¼ cup dark corn syrup
 1 egg
 2 cups salted peanuts

Heat oven to 375°. Line jelly roll pan, 15½ × 10½ × 1 inch, with waxed paper. Cream butter and sugar. Mix in flour, syrup and egg. Stir in peanuts.

Spread in pan. Bake about 25 minutes or until light brown. Loosen layer from sides of pan; invert onto wire rack. Carefully remove paper. Cool; break into pieces.

*Self-rising flour can be used in this recipe.

POLYNESIAN COOKIES

 1 **cup shortening**
1½ **cups sugar**
 1 **egg**
 1 **can (8¼ ounces) crushed pineapple**
3½ **cups all-purpose flour***
 1 **teaspoon soda**
 ½ **teaspoon salt**
 ¼ **teaspoon nutmeg**
 ½ **cup chopped macadamia nuts**

Heat oven to 400°. Mix shortening, sugar and egg. Stir in crushed pineapple (with syrup) and remaining ingredients.

Drop dough by teaspoonfuls about 2 inches apart onto ungreased baking sheet. Bake 8 to 10 minutes or until golden brown and no imprint remains when touched lightly with finger.

About 5 dozen cookies.

**If using self-rising flour, omit soda and salt.*

Substitution

For macadamia nuts: ½ cup chopped walnuts or pecans.

VARIATIONS

■ *Pineapple Coconut Cookies:* Omit nutmeg; stir in 1 cup flaked coconut.

■ *Pineapple Raisin Cookies:* Stir in 1 cup raisins.

Take Care with Your Cookie-baking

☐ Make sure your baking sheets are in good condition—nice and smooth. They should be at least 2 inches narrower and shorter than your oven.
☐ Don't grease unless the recipe tells you so.
☐ Always place cookie dough on a cool sheet.
☐ It's best to bake cookies one sheet at a time, in the center of the oven.
☐ With drop cookies, you can take a trial run: bake a test cookie. If it spreads more than you like, add 1 or 2 tablespoons flour to the dough. If it's too dry or crumbly, add 1 or 2 tablespoons cream or milk.
☐ Don't overbake. Check cookies at the end of the minimum baking time. Even one minute can make a big difference.
☐ When cookies are done, remove from the baking sheet immediately—unless the recipe directs otherwise. Cool on a wire rack.

CHOCOLATE CHIP COOKIES

⅔ **cup shortening**
⅔ **cup butter or margarine, softened**
 1 **cup granulated sugar**
 1 **cup brown sugar (packed)**
 2 **eggs**
 2 **teaspoons vanilla**
 3 **cups all-purpose flour***
 1 **teaspoon soda**
 1 **teaspoon salt**
 1 **cup chopped nuts**
 2 **packages (6 ounces each) semisweet chocolate pieces**

Heat oven to 375°. Mix shortening, butter, sugars, eggs and vanilla. Stir in remaining ingredients. (For a softer, rounder cookie, add ½ cup flour.)

Drop dough by rounded teaspoonfuls 2 inches apart onto ungreased baking sheet. Bake 8 to 10 minutes or until light brown. Cool slightly before removing from baking sheet.

About 7 dozen cookies.

**If using self-rising flour, omit soda and salt.*

VARIATION

■ *Salted Peanut Cookies:* Substitute 2 cups salted peanuts for the chopped nuts and chocolate pieces. Before baking, flatten each cookie with bottom of glass that has been greased and dipped in sugar.

BROWN SUGAR PECAN ROUNDS

 ½ **cup butter or margarine, softened**
1¼ **cups brown sugar (packed)**
 1 **egg**
1¼ **cups all-purpose flour***
 ¼ **teaspoon soda**
 ⅛ **teaspoon salt**
 ½ **cup coarsely chopped pecans**

Heat oven to 350°. Mix butter, brown sugar and egg. Stir in remaining ingredients.

Drop dough by teaspoonfuls about 2 inches apart onto ungreased baking sheet. (Dough will flatten and spread.) Bake 12 to 15 minutes or until set.

About 3 dozen cookies.

**If using self-rising flour, omit soda and salt.*

Fruit Desserts

FRUIT AND CHEESE TRAY

Pictured on page 75.

Arrange a variety of fresh fruit and cheese on a tray. Serve with dessert plates and small knives.

Select fresh fruits in season: apples, bananas, cherries, grapes, oranges, pears, pineapple, raspberries, strawberries, tangerines. Fill in with dates, figs, prunes and shell nuts. As a guide to cheese selection, choose at least one soft, one semisoft and one firm-to-hard cheese, some mild and some sharp. Try one of the following combinations:

Gourmandise (soft; cherry brandy-flavored)
Port du Salut (semisoft; mild to robust)
Swiss (firm to hard; mild, nutty, sweet) or **Fontina** (firm to hard; mellow, scattered "eyes")

Liederkranz (soft; edible crust, pungent)
Bel Paese (semisoft; mild)
Cheddar (firm to hard; mild to very sharp) or **Gruyère** (firm to hard; nutty, sharper than Swiss)

Camembert (soft; edible crust, pungent) or **Brie** (soft; edible crust, pungent)
Roquefort (semisoft; sharp, salty)
Edam or Gouda (firm to hard; inedible casing, mild)

Or make substitutions or additions as desired from the following:

Club (soft; often flavored)
Cream (soft; very mild, chill slightly)
Blue (firm to hard; tangy, sharp)
Gorgonzola (firm to hard; piquant flavor, crumbly)
Kashkaval (firm to hard; salty)

FRUITED SHERBET

Sprinkle cubes of pineapple or other fresh fruit with confectioners' sugar; cover and refrigerate. Just before serving, scoop lime sherbet into individual serving dishes; surround with the fruit.

STRAWBERRIES TO DIP

Wash 1 pint fresh strawberries; do not hull. Chill. To serve, divide berries among individual serving dishes. Pass bowls of sour cream and brown sugar to be spooned onto dishes. Berries are first dipped into sour cream, then into sugar.

4 servings.

STRAWBERRIES ROMANOFF

 1 quart strawberries, hulled
 ½ cup confectioners' sugar
 1 cup chilled whipping cream
 ¼ cup orange-flavored liqueur

Sprinkle strawberries with sugar; stir gently. Cover; refrigerate at least 2 hours.

Just before serving, beat cream in chilled bowl until stiff. Gradually stir in liqueur. Fold in strawberries.

6 servings.

Substitution

For liqueur: ¼ cup orange juice.

MINTED GRAPEFRUIT

 1 can (16 ounces) grapefruit sections
 12 peppermint candy circles, crushed

Mix grapefruit (with syrup) and candy. Cover; refrigerate at least 1 hour.

4 servings.

Substitution

For canned grapefruit sections: 2 medium grapefruit, pared and sectioned (about 2 cups sections and juice).

PEARS AU CHOCOLAT

Chill can of pear halves. For each serving, put 2 well-drained pear halves together with 1 tablespoon canned chocolate frosting in cavity. Stand pear upright in individual serving dish; chill.

Just before serving, melt 1 tablespoon chocolate frosting per serving (in custard cup placed in boiling water); pour on pears.

FRUIT IN SOUR CREAM

2 cups seedless green grapes
1 can (13¼ ounces) pineapple chunks, drained
¼ cup brown sugar (packed)
⅓ cup dairy sour cream

Mix grapes and pineapple. Reserving 1 tablespoon of the brown sugar, stir remaining sugar into sour cream. Toss with fruit; chill. Just before serving, sprinkle with reserved brown sugar.

4 servings.

Substitutions

For fresh grapes: 1 can (16 ounces) seedless grapes, drained.
For sour cream: ⅓ cup unflavored yogurt.

VARIATION

■ *Strawberries in Sour Cream:* Substitute 3 cups fresh strawberry halves (about 1 pint) for the grapes and pineapple.

PINEAPPLE ZIP

2 cans (about 8¼ ounces each) pineapple chunks
2 tablespoons maraschino cherry syrup
½ cup orange juice
¼ cup confectioners' sugar
⅛ teaspoon cinnamon

Mix pineapple (with syrup) and remaining ingredients. Cover; refrigerate at least 1 hour.

4 to 6 servings.

PINEAPPLE DATE DESSERT

Prepare 1 package (14 ounces) date bar mix as directed except—decrease hot water to ¼ cup and stir 1 can (8¼ ounces) crushed pineapple, drained, into date filling. Serve with sweetened whipped cream or frozen whipped topping (thawed).

9 servings.

RUBY-JEWELED PEARS

1 can (16 ounces) whole cranberry sauce
¼ cup sugar
2 tablespoons lemon juice
¼ teaspoon cinnamon
4 pears, pared and cored

Heat oven to 350°. Mix cranberry sauce, sugar, lemon juice and cinnamon in saucepan. Cook over low heat, stirring occasionally, until the sugar is dissolved.

Stand pears upright in ungreased baking pan, 8 × 8 × 2 inches; pour sauce on pears. Bake 30 minutes or until tender, basting occasionally.

4 servings.

HOT FRUIT COMPOTE

1 banana
  Corn syrup
1 jar (30 ounces) fruits for salad, drained
2 tablespoons brown sugar
1 tablespoon butter or margarine

Heat oven to 350°. Slice banana; dip into corn syrup. Arrange all fruit in ungreased baking pan, 13 × 9 × 2 inches. Sprinkle with sugar; dot with butter. Bake 20 minutes. For a topping, mix 1 cup canned vanilla pudding and 2 tablespoons water.

4 to 6 servings.

Substitution

For fruits for salad: 2 cans (17 ounces each) fruits for salad.

BROILED FRUIT KABOBS

Pictured on page 75.

Set oven control at broil and/or 550°. Cut a variety of fresh or canned fruits into uniform pieces, about ¾-inch cubes. (Try pineapple, pitted cooked prunes, peaches, pears, maraschino cherries, bananas or apples.) Alternate fruits on long skewers; place on well-greased rack in broiler pan.

Blend ¼ cup honey and 1½ teaspoons lemon juice; brush on fruit. Broil kabobs about 5 inches from heat 1½ minutes or until light brown. Turn carefully; brush with honey mixture. Broil 1½ minutes longer or until heated through.

APPLE CRISP

Butter Crunch (below)
1 can (21 ounces) apple pie filling
1 teaspoon lemon juice
½ teaspoon cinnamon
1 or 2 drops aromatic bitters, if desired

Prepare Butter Crunch. Heat oven to 450°. Mix remaining ingredients. Place apple mixture in ungreased 9-inch pie pan or in baking dish, 8 × 8 × 2 inches. Sprinkle 1 cup of the Butter Crunch evenly on top. Bake 10 minutes or until golden brown and bubbly. Serve warm. Delicious topped with ice cream.

4 servings.

BUTTER CRUNCH

½ cup butter or margarine
¼ cup brown sugar (packed)
1 cup all-purpose flour*
½ cup chopped pecans, walnuts or coconut

Heat oven to 400°. Mix all ingredients with hands. Spread in ungreased baking pan, 13 × 9 × 2 inches. Bake 15 minutes. Stir with spoon; cool. (Store in covered container in refrigerator.)

*Do not use self-rising flour in this recipe.

CARAMEL PEACH CRISPS

1 can (16 ounces) cling peach halves, drained
2 tablespoons brown sugar
⅔ cup whole wheat flake cereal
¼ cup brown sugar (packed)
3 tablespoons butter or margarine, melted
2 tablespoons raisins
2 tablespoons broken pecans
Vanilla ice cream

Set oven control at broil and/or 550°. Place peach halves cut side up in ungreased baking pan, 8 × 8 × 2 inches; sprinkle with 2 tablespoons brown sugar. Broil peaches 5 inches from heat 2 to 3 minutes or until light brown.

Mix remaining ingredients except ice cream; spoon onto peaches. Broil about 1 minute longer or until mixture is bubbly and brown. Serve with ice cream.

4 to 6 servings.

CHERRY COBBLER

Pictured on page 75.

1 can (21 ounces) cherry pie filling
½ teaspoon almond extract
1 cup buttermilk baking mix
1 tablespoon sugar
¼ cup milk
1 tablespoon soft butter
2 tablespoons toasted slivered blanched almonds

Heat oven to 400°. In 1½-quart casserole, mix pie filling and almond extract. Place in oven 15 minutes or until hot and bubbly.

Mix baking mix, sugar, milk and butter with fork until a soft dough forms; beat vigorously 20 strokes. Stir in almonds. Drop 6 spoonfuls of dough onto hot cherry mixture. Bake 20 to 25 minutes or until topping is light brown. For a touch of tradition, serve with light cream.

6 servings.

VARIATIONS

■ *Blueberry Cobbler:* Omit cherry pie filling and almond extract; substitute 1 can (21 ounces) blueberry pie filling and ½ teaspoon grated orange peel.

■ *Peach Cobbler:* Omit cherry pie filling and almond extract; substitute 1 can (21 ounces) peach pie filling and ½ teaspoon cinnamon.

CHOCOLATE FONDUE

Heat 1 container (16.5 ounces) chocolate frosting over low heat, stirring frequently. Pour into fondue pot or chafing dish to keep warm. Offer pineapple chunks, banana slices, fresh strawberries and cubes of angel food cake to dip into the fondue.

VARIATIONS

■ *Almond Chocolate Fondue:* Stir ½ teaspoon vanilla and ¼ teaspoon almond extract into frosting.

■ *Mint Chocolate Fondue:* Stir ½ teaspoon mint extract into frosting.

Chilled and Frozen Desserts

RASPBERRY-RASPBERRY

Pictured on page 96.

- 1 cup boiling water
- 1 package (3 ounces) raspberry-flavored gelatin
- 4 to 6 ice cubes
- 1 carton (8 ounces) raspberry-flavored yogurt

Pour boiling water on gelatin in large bowl, stirring until gelatin is dissolved. Add ice cubes; stir until gelatin begins to thicken. Remove any remaining ice cubes.

Add yogurt; beat until smooth with rotary beater. Pour into individual serving dishes, glasses or molds. Chill until firm, about 45 minutes. Serve with a dollop of whipped topping.

5 or 6 servings.

Note: Try other gelatin and yogurt combinations.

STRAWBERRY ICE

- 1 package (3 ounces) strawberry-flavored gelatin
- ½ cup sugar
- 1½ cups boiling water
- 1 package (16 ounces) frozen sliced strawberries, partially thawed
- ¼ cup orange juice
- ¼ cup lemon juice

Blend gelatin and sugar; pour boiling water on gelatin mixture in large bowl, stirring until gelatin is dissolved. Stir in remaining ingredients.

Pour into 2 refrigerator trays; freeze until mushy, about 1 hour. Remove from trays; beat until smooth. Return to trays; freeze until firm, about 1 hour.

8 to 10 servings.

FRUIT DESSERT FREEZE

- 1 package (15.4 ounces) creamy white frosting mix
- 2 cups whipping cream
- 1 large banana
- 1 can (8¼ ounces) crushed pineapple, drained
- 1 can (11 ounces) mandarin orange segments, drained
- ⅓ cup halved maraschino cherries, drained
- ⅓ cup cut-up dates
- ⅓ cup chopped pecans, if desired
- 2 tablespoons lemon juice

In small mixer bowl, chill frosting mix (dry) and whipping cream at least 1 hour. Beat until soft peaks form. Slice banana into frosting mixture; fold in remaining ingredients. Pour into 2 refrigerator trays or a baking pan, 9×9×2 inches. Freeze until firm. Remove from freezer 5 minutes before cutting. Cut into squares.

12 servings.

VARIATION

■ *Fruit Salad Freeze:* Fold ⅓ cup mayonnaise into beaten frosting mix and whipping cream.

CHERRIES SUPREME

- ½ cup butter or margarine, softened
- ½ cup brown sugar (packed)
- 1 cup all-purpose flour*
- ½ cup chopped pecans
- ½ gallon vanilla ice cream, softened
- 1 can (21 ounces) cherry pie filling
- 2 tablespoons rum flavoring, if desired

Heat oven to 400°. Mix butter, brown sugar, flour and pecans with hands. Press mixture evenly in bottom of baking pan, 9×9×2 inches. Bake about 12 minutes or until light brown. Crumble with spoon; cool.

Reserving 1 cup of the crumbs, press remaining crumbs evenly in pan. Pack ice cream evenly on crumbs. Sprinkle reserved crumbs on top. Freeze until firm. Just before serving, heat pie filling and rum flavoring; spoon onto each serving.

9 servings.

*Do not use self-rising flour in this recipe.

CREAMY LEMON SHERBET

Pictured at left.

- 1 **can (13 ounces) evaporated milk, chilled**
- 1 **can (6 ounces) frozen lemonade concentrate, partially thawed**
- 5 **drops yellow food color**

Beat chilled milk until stiff. Stir in lemonade concentrate and food color. Pour into 2 refrigerator trays; freeze until firm. If desired, serve with a sprinkling of chopped crystallized ginger.

6 to 8 servings.

COOKIE REFRIGERATOR DESSERT

- **About twenty 2-inch vanilla wafers**
- 1 **envelope (about 1½ ounces) whipped topping mix**
- ½ **cup flaked coconut, if desired**
- 1 **can (17.5 ounces) vanilla pudding**
- ¼ **cup finely chopped nuts**

Arrange vanilla wafers in bottom of ungreased baking pan, 9 × 9 × 2 inches. Prepare whipped topping as directed on package. Fold topping and coconut into pudding; spread on wafers. Sprinkle with nuts. Chill at least 1 hour or until firm.

9 servings.

Substitution

For vanilla pudding: Chocolate pudding.

CHOCOLATE-MINT PARFAITS

- ¼ **cup mint jelly**
- 2 **tablespoons water**
- ½ **cup chilled whipping cream**
- 3 **pints chocolate ice cream**

Heat mint jelly and water until smooth, stirring constantly; cool. In chilled bowl, beat whipping cream until stiff; stir in jelly mixture. Alternate layers of ice cream and whipped cream mixture in parfait glasses or other individual serving dishes. Freeze until firm.

8 servings.

Pictured at left:
Raspberry-Raspberry, Individual Baked Alaska,
Creamy Lemon Sherbet—a trio of happy endings.

PARTY PEACH MELBA

- 1 **can (16 ounces) peach halves, drained Toasted almonds**
- 1 **package (10 ounces) frozen raspberries, partially thawed**
- 1 **pint vanilla ice cream**

Place a peach half in each individual serving dish; sprinkle with almonds. Spoon raspberries on top. Cover; refrigerate at least 1 hour. Just before serving, top each serving with a scoop of ice cream.

5 or 6 servings.

ICE-CREAM WAFFLES

- 1 **package (5 ounces) frozen waffles**
- 1 **pint vanilla ice cream**
- 1 **pint strawberries, sliced and sweetened**

Toast waffles as directed on package. Top each with scoop of ice cream. Spoon berries on ice cream.

6 servings.

Substitution

For fresh strawberries: 1 package (16 ounces) frozen sliced strawberries, partially thawed.

VARIATION

■ *Sundae Waffles:* Omit strawberries. Pour warm chocolate sauce on ice cream; top with nuts.

INDIVIDUAL BAKED ALASKAS

Pictured at left.

- 1 **package sponge shortcakes (4)**
- 1 **pint ice cream**
- 1 **package (7.2 ounces) fluffy white frosting mix**

Cover baking sheet with aluminum foil. Arrange shortcakes on foil. Place scoop of ice cream in each shortcake; freeze at least 1 hour.*

Heat oven to 500°. Prepare frosting as directed on package. Completely cover shortcake and ice cream with frosting, sealing it to foil on baking sheet. Bake on lowest rack in oven 3 to 5 minutes or until frosting is light brown. Serve immediately.

4 servings.

Shortcakes can be frozen up to 24 hours at this point.

Puddings

CHOCOLATE-CHERRY PARFAIT

For each serving, alternate layers of canned chocolate pudding and cherry pie filling in parfait glass or individual serving dish. Garnish with whipped cream and a maraschino cherry.

ROCKY ROAD PUDDING

Pictured on page 75.

 1 **can (17.5 ounces) chocolate pudding**
1½ **cups miniature marshmallows**
     Whipped cream

Mix pudding and marshmallows; pour into individual serving dishes. Garnish with whipped cream.

4 or 5 servings.

FRUIT DELIGHT

1 **can (11 ounces) mandarin orange segments, well drained**
1 **can (13¼ ounces) pineapple chunks, well drained and cut in half**
1 **can (17.5 ounces) vanilla pudding**

Mix all ingredients. Spoon into individual serving dishes. Toasted coconut makes a nice garnish.

8 servings.

FRUIT 'N RICE DESSERT

1 **can (17 ounces) rice pudding**
1 **can (17 ounces) fruit cocktail, well drained**
1 **jar (12 ounces) apricot jam**

Mix rice pudding and fruit cocktail; chill. Just before serving, heat apricot jam until melted, stirring occasionally. Spoon pudding into individual serving dishes and top with apricot sauce.

6 servings.

COCONUT PUDDING

Mix ½ cup flaked coconut and 1 can (17.5 ounces) vanilla pudding. Spoon into individual serving dishes. Garnish with sliced strawberries.

4 servings.

PUDDING-PIE DESSERT

For each serving, spoon ¼ cup apricot, blueberry, cherry, peach or strawberry pie filling into individual serving dish or glass. Top with ½ cup rice pudding. Garnish with a spoonful of pie filling.

4 servings.

RICH VANILLA PUDDING

1 **cup dairy sour cream**
1 **can (17.5 ounces) vanilla pudding**
    Canned sliced peaches, drained

Fold sour cream into pudding; pour into individual serving dishes. Top with peaches.

5 or 6 servings.

LEMON PUDDING SHELLS

3 **egg whites**
¼ **teaspoon cream of tartar**
¾ **cup sugar**
1 **package (3¼ ounces) lemon pudding and pie filling**
1 **cup sweetened whipped cream**
8 **fresh strawberries**

Heat oven to 275°. Cover baking sheet with heavy brown paper. In small mixer bowl, beat egg whites and cream of tartar until foamy. Beat in sugar, 1 tablespoon at a time; continue beating until stiff and glossy. Do not underbeat.

Drop meringue by ⅓ cupfuls onto brown paper. Shape mounds into circles with back of spoon, building up sides. Bake 1 hour. Turn off oven; leave meringues in oven with door closed 1½ hours. Remove from oven; finish cooling meringues away from draft. Cook pudding as directed on package; cool. Fill shells with pudding. Top with whipped cream and a strawberry.

8 servings.

Beverages

DEMITASSE

Prepare coffee, using ¼ cup ground coffee for each ¾ cup water. Serve with a twist of lemon peel. Sugar may be used but cream is usually shunned.

2 servings (about ⅓ cup each).

INSTANT DEMITASSE

Measure ½ cup instant coffee into heatproof container. Stir in 1 quart boiling water. Cover; let stand 5 minutes.

12 servings (about ⅓ cup each).

MOCHA DESSERT COFFEE

For each serving, place 1 to 2 tablespoons canned chocolate frosting in cup. Fill with hot coffee; stir until blended. If desired, garnish with whipped topping.

RED-HOT CINNAMON COFFEE

For each serving, place 1 tablespoon red cinnamon candies in mug. Fill with hot coffee; stir. Serve with a cinnamon stick.

CAFÉ MEXICAN

- ⅛ teaspoon cinnamon
- ⅛ teaspoon nutmeg
- 1 cup frozen whipped topping (thawed)
- 2 cups hot strong coffee

Fold spices into whipped topping. Serve coffee in demitasse cups and top with the spiced whipped topping.

6 servings (about ⅓ cup each).

CALIFORNIA COFFEE

For each serving, pour 1 ounce (2 tablespoons) brandy into mug. Fill ⅔ full with hot strong coffee. Top with a small scoop of chocolate ice cream.

IRISH COFFEE

- 1 cup chilled whipping cream
- ¼ cup confectioners' sugar
- 1 teaspoon vanilla
- ¾ cup ground coffee
- 3 cups water
- 4 ounces (½ cup) Irish whiskey or brandy
- 4 to 8 teaspoons granulated sugar

In chilled bowl, beat cream, confectioners' sugar and vanilla until stiff; refrigerate.

Prepare coffee, using the ¾ cup ground coffee and 3 cups water.

Heat 4 mugs by rinsing with boiling water; drain. Mix 1 ounce (2 tablespoons) whiskey and 1 to 2 tablespoons granulated sugar in each mug; add hot coffee. Top with the whipped cream.

4 servings (¾ cup each).

COFFEE À LA MODE

For each serving, fill mugs about ¾ full with steaming hot strong coffee. Top with a small scoop of vanilla or coffee ice cream. Serve at once.

SPICED TEA

- 4 cups boiling water
- 4 teaspoons loose tea
- 6 whole cloves, broken into pieces
- ½ teaspoon dried orange peel
- ⅛ teaspoon cinnamon

Pour boiling water over tea, cloves, orange peel and cinnamon in heatproof container. Cover tightly; let steep 3 to 5 minutes. Stir and strain.

6 servings (⅔ cup each).

ICE-CREAM SODA

For each serving, place 2 to 3 tablespoons any flavor syrup (or ice-cream topping) or ¼ cup crushed fruit with 1 teaspoon sugar in tall glass. Fill ½ full with chilled sparkling water. Top with a scoop of ice cream; stir vigorously. Fill with sparkling water.

FRUIT FIZZ

For each serving, place ¼ cup chilled pineapple juice and 1 scoop vanilla ice cream in tall glass. Fill with chilled sparkling water; stir lightly.

Substitution

For pineapple juice: ¼ cup grape, cherry or raspberry juice or cranberry cocktail.

STRAWBERRY CREAM

For each serving, blend ½ pint vanilla ice cream (1 cup) and ½ cup chilled strawberry soda in blender or with rotary beater.

ORANGE FREEZE

For each serving, place 2 tablespoons frozen orange juice concentrate (thawed) and 1 scoop vanilla ice cream in tall glass. Fill with chilled ginger ale; stir lightly. Serve with a halved orange slice.

ORANGE FROST SODA

Pictured on page 75.

  1 quart orange sherbet
  2 bottles (14 ounces each)
    carbonated orange beverage, chilled

Place 2 scoops orange sherbet in each of 5 tall glasses. Fill with orange beverage.

5 servings.

CRANBERRY FROST

For each serving, place 1 scoop lime sherbet in tall glass. Fill with chilled cranberry cocktail.

Substitution

For lime sherbet: Lemon or orange sherbet.

CREAMY PEACH CUP

  1 package (12 ounces) frozen
    sliced peaches
  ¼ cup canned vanilla pudding
  ¾ cup milk
  ¼ teaspoon almond extract

Thaw peaches just until they can be removed from package; cut into chunks. Pour into blender; blend until thoroughly chopped. Add remaining ingredients; mix until smooth. Serve immediately in chilled cups or individual serving dishes.

3 or 4 servings.

Pictured at right:

TOP
  Shrimp Bisque
  Oven French Toast
  Individual Submarine Sandwich

CENTER
  Home-style Scrambled Eggs
  Rolled Egg/Canadian-style Bacon/Jam Crumpet
  Honey Bee Ambrosia

BOTTOM
  Tomato Shortcake
  Soup 'n Cereal
  Hash and Cheese Grill

Breakfasts and Lunches

Breakfast Fruits

HONEY BEE AMBROSIA

Pictured on page 101.

- **4 medium oranges, chilled**
- **1 medium banana**
- **½ cup orange juice**
- **¼ cup honey**
- **2 tablespoons lemon juice**
- **¼ cup flaked coconut**

Pare oranges and cut into thin slices. Peel banana and cut into slices. Mix fruits carefully. Blend orange juice, honey and lemon juice; pour on fruit. Sprinkle with coconut.

4 to 6 servings.

FRUIT WITH YOGURT

- **1 can (30 ounces) fruit cocktail, drained**
- **½ cup unflavored yogurt**
- **2 tablespoons honey**
- **2 teaspoons lemon juice**
- **Dash aromatic bitters, if desired**

Spoon fruit into individual serving dishes. Blend yogurt, honey, lemon juice and bitters; pour over fruit. Especially good when served with Almond Flatbread (page 71).

4 or 5 servings.

Substitutions

For fruit cocktail: 1 can (30 ounces) apricot halves or peach halves or about 4 cups cut-up fresh fruit.
For yogurt: ½ cup dairy sour cream.

PAPAYA

Cut 2 large ripe papayas in half lengthwise; remove seeds. Pare and cut into slices. Serve with lime wedges.

4 servings.

FROZEN FRUIT SLICES

Remove wrapping from 1 package (16 ounces) frozen melon balls. Cut frozen fruit into ⅜- to ½-inch slices with serrated knife. Place slices on salad plates with curly endive or sprigs of watercress or parsley.

4 or 5 servings.

Substitution

For melon balls: 1 package (10 ounces) frozen peach slices, 1 package (10 ounces) frozen strawberry halves or 1 can (13½ ounces) frozen pineapple chunks.

STRAWBERRY-RHUBARB COMPOTE

- **½ cup water**
- **1 package (16 ounces) frozen rhubarb**
- **2 tablespoons sugar**
- **2 cups fresh strawberries**
- **⅛ teaspoon ginger**

Heat water to boiling; stir in rhubarb and sugar. Reduce heat; simmer 5 minutes, breaking fruit apart with fork. Remove from heat; stir in strawberries and ginger. Serve warm or cold.

Remember this fruit refresher as a first course for dinner, too.

6 servings.

MELON AND PROSCIUTTO

Cut a ripe cantaloupe, casaba, honeydew or Spanish melon (about 3 pounds) in half; scoop out seeds and fibers. Cut each half into 6 lengthwise wedges. Remove rind. Cut crosswise slits 1½ inches apart in each melon wedge.

Cut ¼ pound sliced prosciutto (Italian ham) into 1-inch strips. Place several strips of ham on each wedge; push ham into slits.

12 servings.

VARIATION

■ *Bite-size Melon and Prosciutto:* Cut pared melon into bite-size pieces. Wrap each piece in strips of prosciutto; secure with picks.

DRIED FRUIT COMPOTE

- **1 package (10 ounces) mixed dried fruit**
  One 3-inch stick cinnamon
- **¼ cup brown sugar (packed)**
- **3 slices lemon**
- **2 cups water**
- **1 can (21 ounces) cherry pie filling**

Mix dried fruit, cinnamon stick, sugar, lemon slices and water in saucepan. Heat to boiling, stirring occasionally. Reduce heat; simmer uncovered 30 minutes. Stir in cherry pie filling. Serve warm or cold. This fruit combo also makes a particularly nice accompaniment for ham or roast beef.

4 to 6 servings.

VARIATION

■ *Currant-Raspberry Compote:* Omit cherry pie filling. Drain cooked fruit, reserving liquid. Measure reserved liquid and, if necessary, add enough water to measure 2½ cups. Prepare 1 package (4¾ ounces) currant-raspberry-flavored dessert mix as directed on package for fruit sauce except—substitute the reserved 2½ cups liquid for the water.

CINNAMON FRUITS

Drain 1 can (16 ounces) peaches or pears, reserving ½ cup syrup. In small saucepan, heat reserved syrup and ¼ cup red cinnamon candies to boiling; boil 1 minute. Remove from heat. Cover tightly; let stand 10 minutes or until candies are dissolved. Stir in fruit. Serve warm or chilled.

4 servings.

HOT BREAKFAST FRUITS

- **½ cup butter or margarine**
- **¼ cup brown sugar (packed)**
- **1 tablespoon lemon juice**
- **1 can (30 ounces) fruits for salad, drained**

Melt butter in medium skillet over low heat; blend in sugar and lemon juice. Cook until smooth and bubbly. Stir in fruit; heat through.

Nice to serve on oatmeal or farina. Good for dessert, too—on rice pudding, custard or ice cream.

4 or 5 servings.

CRUNCHY BROILED GRAPEFRUIT

- **2 grapefruit, halved**
- **1 cup whole wheat flake cereal, crushed**
- **⅓ cup brown sugar (packed)**
- **¼ cup butter or margarine, melted**

Remove seeds from grapefruit halves. Cut around edges and sections to loosen; remove centers. Mix cereal, sugar and butter; spread on grapefruit.

Set oven control at broil and/or 550°. Broil grapefruit 5 inches from heat 3 to 4 minutes or until golden brown.

4 servings.

BROILED HONEY GRAPEFRUIT

- **2 grapefruit, halved**
- **¼ cup honey**
- **10 drops aromatic bitters**

Remove seeds from grapefruit halves. Cut around edges and sections to loosen; remove centers. Mix honey and bitters; spoon about 1 tablespoon honey mixture on each grapefruit half.

Set oven control at broil and/or 550°. Broil grapefruit 5 inches from heat about 5 minutes.

4 servings.

MARSHMALLOW APRICOTS

Heat oven to 400°. Divide 1 can (17 ounces) apricot halves among 4 or 5 individual ovenproof dishes (about 3 apricot halves and 1 tablespoon syrup per dish). Top each with 6 to 8 miniature marshmallows. Bake 5 minutes or until puffed.

4 or 5 servings.

BAKED BANANAS

Heat oven to 375°. For each serving, peel a large firm banana and cut lengthwise in half. Place halves cut side down in buttered baking dish. Brush with lemon juice. Sprinkle each half with ½ teaspoon grated lemon peel and ½ tablespoon brown sugar. Drizzle each banana with ½ tablespoon butter, melted. Bake 20 minutes. Serve warm. Top with ice cream, for dessert or breakfast.

Cereals

MOCK APPLE DUMPLINGS

2 cups whole wheat flake cereal, crushed
2 tablespoons sugar
⅛ teaspoon salt
⅛ teaspoon nutmeg
⅛ teaspoon cinnamon
3 cups applesauce
    Milk

Mix cereal, sugar, salt, nutmeg and cinnamon. Spoon applesauce into individual serving dishes. Sprinkle cereal mixture on applesauce. Serve with milk.

4 servings.

SOUP 'N CEREAL

Pictured on page 101.

½ soup can milk
½ soup can water
1 can (10¾ ounces) condensed tomato soup
¼ teaspoon salt
    Favorite unsweetened dry cereal

In saucepan, gradually stir milk and water into soup and salt. Heat through over low heat, stirring frequently. Serve on cereal immediately.

3 servings.

FRUITED HOT CEREAL

Prepare cereal as directed on package except— when heating water to boiling, add one of the following for each serving:

2 tablespoons raisins
4 to 5 dried apricot halves, cut up
4 to 5 prunes, cut up
3 to 4 dates, cut up

HOT CEREAL STIR-INS

Prepare your favorite hot cereal as directed on package except—for each serving, stir in one of the following:

1 teaspoon fruit-flavored gelatin (swirled in)
¼ cup miniature marshmallows
1 to 2 tablespoons maple syrup, light molasses or honey
1 tablespoon instant cocoa mix
1 to 2 tablespoons jam, jelly or marmalade
2 tablespoons brown sugar
2 tablespoons applesauce and 1 tablespoon brown sugar
2 tablespoons mandarin orange segments and 1 tablespoon brown sugar

CEREAL TOPPINGS

Try one of these flavored milks on your favorite unsweetened cereal. To ¾ cup milk in blender add one of the following:

¼ banana, cut up
2 teaspoons sugar and 1 teaspoon powdered instant coffee
½ teaspoon sugar-sweetened soft drink mix
1 or 2 canned peach halves
1 tablespoon peanut butter and 1 teaspoon sugar

CEREAL SWEETENERS

Substitute one of the following for sugar on your favorite unsweetened cereal:

Mixture of 2 teaspoons sugar and 1 teaspoon cinnamon
Brown sugar
Maple syrup
Ice-cream sundae topping
Instant cocoa mix
Fruit-flavored gelatin
Jam or jelly
Colored sugars

Eggs

SOFT-COOKED EGGS

Place eggs in saucepan; add enough cold water to come at least 1 inch above eggs. Heat rapidly to boiling. Remove from heat. Cover tightly; let stand 1 to 3 minutes, depending on desired doneness.

Immediately cool eggs in cold water several seconds to prevent further cooking. Cut eggs in half; scoop from shell.

HARD-COOKED EGGS

Place eggs in saucepan; add enough cold water to come at least 1 inch above eggs. Heat rapidly to boiling. Remove from heat. Cover tightly; let stand 25 minutes.

Immediately cool eggs in cold water to prevent further cooking. Tap egg to crackle shell. Roll between hands to loosen shell, then peel. Hold egg under running cold water to help ease off shell.

FRIED EGGS

In heavy skillet, heat butter or bacon fat (⅛ inch deep) until just hot enough to sizzle a drop of water. Break each egg into a measuring cup or saucer; carefully slip eggs one at a time into skillet. Immediately reduce heat to low.

Cook slowly, spooning butter on eggs until whites are set and a film forms over yolks (sunny-side up). Or when whites are set, turn eggs over gently and cook until desired doneness.

VARIATION

■ *Poached-fried Eggs:* Heat just enough butter or bacon fat to grease skillet. Cook eggs over low heat until edges turn white. Add ½ teaspoon water for 1 egg, decreasing the proportion slightly for each additional egg. Cover tightly.

POACHED EGGS

In saucepan or skillet, heat water, bouillon or milk (1½ to 2 inches) to boiling; reduce to simmer. Break each egg into a measuring cup or saucer; carefully slip eggs one at a time into water. (Eggs shouldn't touch each other while cooking.)

Cook 3 to 5 minutes or until desired doneness. Lift eggs from water with slotted spatula. Season with salt and pepper.

Note: To poach eggs in an egg poacher, pour water into poacher to just below bottom of egg cups; heat water to boiling. Butter metal egg cups; break eggs into cups. Set egg cups in frame over boiling water. Cover tightly; steam 3 to 5 minutes or until desired doneness.

BAKED (SHIRRED) EGGS

Heat oven to 325°. For each serving, break an egg carefully into buttered 5- or 6-ounce baking dish. Season with salt and pepper. If desired, top each egg with 1 tablespoon milk or half-and-half, dot with soft butter or sprinkle with 1 tablespoon shredded Cheddar cheese.

Bake eggs uncovered 15 to 18 minutes, depending on desired doneness and depth of baking dish. Whites should be set, but yolks soft. Serve in baking dish.

EGGS ON CORNED BEEF HASH

  1 can (15 ounces) corned beef hash
  6 eggs
    Salt and pepper
⅓ cup shredded Cheddar cheese

Heat oven to 350°. In each of six 5- or 6-ounce baking dishes, press about ¼ cup hash against bottom and side. Break an egg on hash in each dish. Season with salt and pepper. Sprinkle each with about 1 tablespoon cheese. Bake uncovered 20 to 25 minutes, depending on desired doneness.

6 servings.

GOLDEN EGGS ON TOAST

1 can (11 ounces) condensed Cheddar
   cheese soup
⅓ cup milk
6 hard-cooked eggs, sliced
6 slices toast

Heat soup and milk, stirring constantly. Gently stir in egg slices; heat through. Spoon on toast. For extra color and flavor, garnish with snipped chives and crisply fried bacon.

4 to 6 servings.

SCRAMBLED EGGS

For each serving, break 2 eggs into bowl; add 2 tablespoons milk or cream, ¼ teaspoon salt and dash pepper. Mix with fork, stirring thoroughly for a uniform color, or mixing just slightly if streaks of white and yellow are preferred.

Heat ½ tablespoon butter or margarine in skillet over medium heat until just hot enough to sizzle a drop of water. Pour egg mixture into skillet.

As mixture begins to set at bottom and side, gently lift cooked portions with spatula so that thin, uncooked portion can flow to bottom. Avoid constant stirring. Cook until eggs are thickened throughout but still moist, about 3 to 5 minutes.

VARIATIONS

■ *Creamy Scrambled Eggs:* Cook egg mixture in top of double boiler over simmering, not boiling, water. Stir occasionally until thick and creamy.

■ *Flavored Scrambled Eggs:* For each serving, stir one of the following into egg mixture in bowl:

2 tablespoons shredded Cheddar,
   Monterey (Jack) or Swiss cheese
2 tablespoons chopped mushrooms
2 tablespoons snipped chives
2 tablespoons snipped parsley
2 tablespoons crisply fried and
   crumbled bacon*
2 tablespoons finely shredded dried beef*
2 tablespoons chopped cooked ham*

*Omit salt in egg mixture.

HOME-STYLE SCRAMBLED EGGS

Pictured on page 101.

4 eggs
1 tablespoon instant minced onion
¾ teaspoon salt
3 tablespoons water
¼ cup butter or margarine
1 cup diced tomatoes
1 cup diced cooked potatoes
1 cup diced zucchini

Beat eggs, onion, salt and water. Melt butter in large skillet over medium heat; cook and stir vegetables in butter 2 minutes. Pour on egg mixture.

As mixture begins to set at bottom and side, gently lift cooked portions with spatula so that thin, uncooked portion can flow to bottom. Avoid constant stirring. Cook until eggs are thickened throughout but still moist, 3 to 5 minutes.

3 servings.

Substitutions

For instant onion: 3 tablespoons minced onion.
For zucchini: ½ cup chopped green pepper.

VARIATION

■ *Eggs Mexicali:* Decrease salt to ½ teaspoon. Omit instant onion and vegetables; stir ⅔ cup crushed corn chips into butter. Serve with hot chili relish.

ROLLED EGG

Pictured on page 101.

For each Rolled Egg, beat 1 egg and ⅛ teaspoon salt until foamy. Melt 2 teaspoons butter, margarine or bacon fat in hot 10-inch skillet; rotate pan to coat bottom with butter. Pour egg into skillet; slowly rotate pan to spread mixture into thin circle. Cook over medium heat about 2 minutes. Loosen edge; roll up, using small spatula and fork.

When preparing more than one, keep Rolled Eggs warm on ungreased baking sheet in 275° oven. Nice served with a cheese or mushroom sauce.

VARIATION

■ *Cheese Egg Roll:* Before rolling circle, sprinkle with 1 tablespoon Parmesan cheese.

Breakfast Meats

FINNAN HADDIE

- 1 package (16 ounces) frozen finnan
  haddie, thawed
- ¼ cup butter or margarine

Cut fish into serving pieces. Melt butter in skillet. Add fish; reduce heat. Cover tightly; simmer 30 minutes or until fish flakes easily with a fork. To serve, spoon butter over fish.

Traditionally served on buttered toast—but why not try an English muffin and cinnamon apple rings.

4 servings.

Substitution

For finnan haddie: 1 package (16 ounces) frozen wall-eye pike, Northern pike or pollack. Rinse under cold water to remove wrapping. Let fish stand 5 minutes, then saw into serving pieces. Brush with 2 tablespoons liquid smoke; add to butter in skillet. Cover tightly; simmer 30 minutes.

FISH STICK BREAKFAST

- 1 package (16 ounces) frozen fish sticks
- 1 can (8¼ ounces) sliced pineapple, drained
- 2 tablespoons cranberry-orange relish
- 4 English muffins, split and toasted

Arrange fish sticks and pineapple slices on lightly buttered baking sheet. Fill each pineapple slice with a rounded teaspoonful of cranberry-orange relish.

Set oven control at broil and/or 550°. Broil fish sticks and pineapple slices 5 inches from heat about 5 minutes or until fish sticks are golden. Serve with English muffins. And don't forget to serve this treat for lunch or dinner sometime.

4 servings.

SAUSAGE (Uncooked Smoked or Fresh)

To Panfry: Place sausage links or patties in cold skillet. Add 2 to 4 tablespoons water. Cover tightly; cook slowly 5 to 8 minutes, depending on size or thickness of sausages. Uncover; cook until well done, turning to brown evenly.

To Bake: Arrange sausages in single layer in ungreased shallow baking pan. Bake uncovered in 400° oven 20 to 30 minutes or until well done, turning sausages to brown evenly. Drain off fat as it accumulates.

YORKSHIRE SAUSAGE

- 1 cup all-purpose flour*
- ½ teaspoon salt
- 1 cup milk
- 2 eggs
- 1 package (10 ounces) brown and serve
  smoked sausages (10)

Heat oven to 425°. Butter baking pan, 9×9×2 inches. Mix flour, salt, milk and eggs with rotary beater just until smooth. (Do not overbeat.) Pour into pan.

Arrange sausages on batter. Bake 25 minutes or until puffed and brown. Delicious with warm applesauce. For a complete breakfast add a glass of orange juice and a glass of milk.

4 or 5 servings.

*Do not use self-rising flour in this recipe.

Substitution

For salt: ½ teaspoon favorite seasoned salt.

Merry Up the Menu—Maybe Then They'll Eat

Soup for breakfast? Why not! It's filling . . . and fast. Try any of your favorites (and be sure to look over the selection on pages 114-115). And how about breakfast sandwiches? Plain old peanut butter goes over big with You Know Who, and Breakfast Burgers (page 109) are sure to draw the teen-agers to the scene. And Denvers (page 117). They ought to give you a full table. Another day, surprise them with Baked Meatballs (page 16) or Ovenfried Fillets (page 45). Morning monotony? Not for you or your family!

CHICKEN LIVERS WITH MUSHROOMS

¼ cup butter or margarine
½ pound chicken livers, halved
¼ pound fresh mushrooms, sliced
¼ teaspoon salt
2 teaspoons Worcestershire sauce

Melt butter in large skillet; brown livers. Push livers to one side. Add mushrooms; cook and stir until mushrooms are light brown. Mix livers and mushrooms.

Sprinkle with salt and Worcestershire sauce. Reduce heat. Cover tightly; simmer 5 minutes or until livers are done.

Serve with an omelet or scrambled eggs for a special brunch.

2 or 3 servings.

Substitution

For fresh mushrooms: 1 can (4 ounces) mushroom stems and pieces, drained.

BREAKFAST BURGERS

1 pound ground beef
¼ cup applesauce
1 teaspoon salt
1 teaspoon Worcestershire sauce
½ teaspoon allspice

Mix all ingredients. Shape mixture by tablespoonfuls into 2-inch patties. Cook in skillet over medium high heat, about 2 to 3 minutes on each side.

6 to 8 servings.

VARIATION

■ *Baked Breakfast Burgers:* Shape mixture into 5 patties, about 3 inches in diameter and ½ inch thick. Bake in 350° oven 20 minutes. Serve on a bun or toasted French bread.

Pictured at left:
Chicken Livers with Mushrooms

MEAT 'N POTATO ROLL-UPS

Instant mashed potatoes (enough for 4 servings)
1 tablespoon finely chopped green pepper
¼ teaspoon instant chopped onion
½ teaspoon prepared mustard
8 slices large bologna

Heat oven to 350°. Prepare mashed potatoes as directed on package. Stir in green pepper, onion and mustard.

Place about ¼ cup potato mixture on each bologna slice; roll up and secure with wooden pick. Place on ungreased baking sheet. Bake 10 to 15 minutes.

An unusual lunch, brunch or hearty breakfast served with Frozen Fruit Slices (page 102).

4 servings.

BACON

To Panfry: Place bacon slices in cold skillet. Cook over low heat 8 to 10 minutes, turning to brown evenly.

To Bake: Place separated slices of bacon on rack in broiler pan. Bake in 400° oven 10 minutes or until brown. Do not turn.

To Broil: Place separated slices of bacon on rack in broiler pan. Set oven control at broil and/or 550°. Broil bacon 3 inches from heat until brown, about 2 minutes. Turn slices; broil 1 minute longer.

CANADIAN-STYLE BACON

To Panfry: Place ⅛-inch slices of Canadian-style bacon in cold skillet. Cook over low heat 8 to 10 minutes, turning to brown evenly.

To Bake: If necessary, remove casing from 2-pound piece of Canadian-style bacon. Place bacon fat side up on rack in open shallow baking pan. Insert meat thermometer so tip is in center of bacon. Bake uncovered in 325° oven 1 to 1¼ hours or until thermometer registers 160°.

To Broil: Place ¼-inch slices Canadian-style bacon on rack in broiler pan. Set oven control at broil and/or 550°. Broil bacon 2 to 3 inches from heat until brown, about 3 minutes. Turn slices; broil 3 minutes longer.

Breakfast Breads

FLAVORED OVEN TOAST

Heat oven to 400°. Cut unsliced loaf of bread into desired number of 1-inch slices. Spread both sides of slices with butter. Arrange on ungreased baking sheet. Bake 10 to 12 minutes or until golden brown. Sprinkle with instant cocoa, orange-flavored instant breakfast drink (dry) or fruit-flavored gelatin.

BREAKFAST HOT SWEETS

Heat oven to 400°. Cut unsliced nut bread into desired number of ½-inch slices. Spread with soft butter or margarine. Arrange buttered side up on ungreased baking sheet. Bake 6 to 8 minutes or until light brown.

JAM CRUMPETS

Pictured on page 101 with the Rolled Egg.

- 6 English muffins, split
- ¼ cup soft butter or margarine
- ¼ cup jam or preserves
- ¼ cup brown sugar (packed)
- ¼ cup flaked coconut or sliced almonds

Heat oven to 450°. Spread cut surface of each muffin half with 1 teaspoon each butter and jam. Sprinkle with brown sugar and coconut. Bake on ungreased baking sheet 5 minutes or until bubbly and brown.

12 crumpets.

JAM GRILL

For each serving, spread 1 slice bread with 2 tablespoons strawberry or raspberry jam; top with second slice bread. Spread outside of sandwich with about 1 tablespoon soft butter or margarine. Cook on both sides in skillet or on grill. Sprinkle with confectioners' sugar.

ORANGE ROLLS

- 1 loaf (1 pound) frozen bread dough
  Salad oil
- 3 tablespoons soft butter or margarine
- 1 tablespoon grated orange peel
- 2 tablespoons orange juice
- 1½ cups confectioners' sugar

Brush frozen loaf with oil. Place on lightly greased baking sheet; cover and thaw up to 12 hours in refrigerator or about 3 hours at room temperature.

Beat butter, orange peel, juice and confectioners' sugar until creamy and smooth. On lightly floured board, roll dough into rectangle, 15×8 inches. Spread with half the orange mixture; roll up, beginning at wide side. Pinch edge of dough into roll to seal well. Stretch to make even.

Cut roll into 15 slices. Place slightly apart in greased baking pan, 13×9×2 inches, or in greased muffin cups. Let rise until double, about 1 hour.

Heat oven to 350°. Bake 35 to 40 minutes or until golden brown. While warm, remove from pan and frost with remaining orange filling.

15 rolls.

VARIATIONS

■ *Caramel Rolls:* Before rolling dough, melt ¼ cup butter or margarine; stir in ½ cup brown sugar (packed), 2 tablespoons corn syrup and ½ cup pecan halves and spread over bottom of baking pan. Omit orange peel, juice and confectioners' sugar. Spread rectangle with 3 tablespoons butter; sprinkle with mixture of ¼ cup granulated sugar and 2 teaspoons cinnamon. After baking, immediately turn pan upside down on large tray. Let pan remain on a minute so caramel drizzles over rolls.

■ *Cinnamon Rolls:* Omit orange peel, orange juice and confectioners' sugar. Spread rectangle with 3 tablespoons butter and sprinkle with mixture of ¼ cup granulated sugar, 2 teaspoons cinnamon and ½ cup chopped nuts. While rolls are warm, frost with mixture of 1½ cups confectioners' sugar and 1 tablespoon milk.

PEANUT BUTTER AND JELLY COFFEE CAKE

2 cups buttermilk baking mix
2 tablespoons sugar
¼ cup creamy peanut butter
⅔ cup milk
1 egg
½ cup favorite jam or jelly

Heat oven to 400°. Grease layer pan, 9 × 1½ inches. Mix baking mix and sugar; cut in peanut butter. Mix in milk and egg; beat vigorously ½ minute.

Spread in pan; spread with jam. Bake 20 to 25 minutes or until light brown.

9 servings.

Substitution

For jam or jelly: ½ cup orange marmalade.

HAM WAFFLES

2 cups buttermilk baking mix
2 tablespoons shortening, melted, or salad oil
1⅓ cups milk
1 egg
1 package (3 ounces) smoked pressed ham

Heat waffle iron. Beat baking mix, shortening, milk and egg with rotary beater until smooth. Stir in ham. Pour batter from cup or pitcher onto center of hot waffle iron. Bake about 5 minutes or until steaming stops. Lift waffle carefully with fork.

Three 9-inch waffles.

Note: To freeze waffles, bake, cool and wrap individually in foil. To reheat, unwrap and arrange on baking sheet. Bake in 400° oven 8 to 10 minutes or until hot.

VARIATION

■ *Orange-Nut Waffles:* Omit ham. Substitute orange juice for the milk and stir ¾ cup finely chopped nuts into batter.

Starting with a mix... PANCAKE VARIATIONS

Prepare Pancakes as directed on buttermilk baking mix package except—try one of the following tasty variations:

■ *Cheese:* Fold in ½ to 1½ cups shredded sharp cheese.

■ *Corn:* Fold in 1 cup drained whole kernel corn.

■ *Ham:* Fold in 1 to 1½ cups ground or chopped cooked ham.

OVEN FRENCH TOAST

Pictured on page 101.

4 slices white bread, 1 inch thick
3 eggs, slightly beaten
¾ cup milk
1 tablespoon sugar
¼ teaspoon salt

Heat oven to 500°. Arrange bread in ungreased baking dish, 13½ × 9 × 2 inches. Beat eggs, milk, sugar and salt. Pour egg mixture on bread; turn each slice to coat well.

With pancake turner, arrange bread on greased baking sheet. Bake about 8 minutes. Turn and bake about 8 minutes longer or until golden brown. Serve with warm cranberry sauce.

4 servings.

Note: The toast can also be cooked in buttered skillet or on a griddle.

Substitution

For 1-inch slices bread: 4 to 6 ½-inch slices white bread or 8 1¼-inch slices French bread; cover baking dish and refrigerate at least 8 hours.

VARIATION

■ *Waffled French Toast:* Heat waffle iron. Use 1-inch or ½-inch slices white bread; arrange on hot ungreased waffle iron and bake 3 to 5 minutes or until golden brown.

Note: To freeze Waffled French Toast, bake, cool and wrap individually in foil. To reheat, unwrap and arrange on baking sheet. Heat in 400° oven 8 to 10 minutes.

Breakfast Beverages

BREAKFAST PUNCH

1 cup orange juice, chilled
½ cup lemon juice, chilled
2 cups apple cider, chilled
¼ cup sugar

Stir juices and sugar until sugar is dissolved. Pour over ice cubes. Garnish with mint leaves.

4 or 5 servings.

MULLED APRICOT NECTAR

1 can (46 ounces) apricot nectar
½ lemon, sliced
2 cinnamon sticks
15 whole cloves
8 whole allspice

Mix all ingredients in heavy saucepan; heat to boiling. Reduce heat; simmer gently 5 minutes. Remove from heat. Cover tightly; allow to stand 30 minutes. Strain. Reheat before serving.

12 servings (½ cup each).

SPARKLING ORANGE JUICE

For each serving, fill glass with 2 parts orange juice and 1 part chilled carbonated lemon beverage. Float a half-slice of orange or a fresh mint sprig in each glass.

TOMATO BOUILLON

¾ cup tomato juice
¼ cup water
1 teaspoon instant beef bouillon

Heat all ingredients to boiling over medium-high heat, stirring occasionally. Serve hot or cold.

2 servings.

SUNNY SIPPER

¼ cup honey
½ cup orange juice
  Juice of 1 lemon
1 can (6 ounces) evaporated milk (undiluted)
1 can (12 ounces) apricot nectar

Blend honey, orange juice and lemon juice. Add evaporated milk and apricot nectar; beat until foamy. Chill. Just before serving, beat again. Serve in small cups.

4 servings.

BANANA ORANGE FROST

1 ripe banana
½ cup orange juice
½ cup cold milk
½ pint (1 cup) orange sherbet

Mash banana with fork; stir in orange juice. Beat with rotary beater or in blender. Add milk and orange sherbet; beat until smooth. Serve on scoops of orange sherbet. Garnish with an orange slice.

2 or 3 servings.

ORANGE EGGNOG

1 can (6 ounces) frozen orange juice concentrate (thawed)
2 cups milk
2 cups eggnog

Beat orange juice and milk with rotary beater or in blender. Stir in eggnog. A sprinkling of colored sugar or nutmeg makes a pretty topping.

4 servings.

COCOA-CEREAL MILK SHAKE

1 cup milk
1 pint chocolate ice cream, slightly softened
2 cups chocolate-flavored corn puff cereal
1 tablespoon malted milk powder, if desired

Measure all ingredients into blender. Cover; blend at high speed 10 seconds; stop blender and scrape down sides. Cover; blend 20 seconds. Complete this breakfast with Honey Bee Ambrosia (page 102).

2 servings.

FLAVORED MILKS

For each serving, add one of the following to a tall glass:

- **2 tablespoons caramel syrup**
- **1 maraschino cherry and 2 tablespoons maraschino cherry juice**
- **1 tablespoon chocolate syrup and 1 tablespoon chunky peanut butter**
- **1 to 2 tablespoons chocolate syrup, cocoa mix or ice-cream topping**
- **1 tablespoon honey, 1 tablespoon grape juice, orange juice or lemonade or limeade concentrate**

Fill glass with milk and stir thoroughly. Serve immediately.

CHOCOLATE MILK SHAKE

Measure ¼ cup Chocolate Fudge Sauce (below) and ¾ cup milk into blender. Cover; blend 2 seconds. Add 3 scoops vanilla ice cream; blend at low speed 5 seconds. (Or, beat all ingredients with rotary beater.)

1 serving.

CHOCOLATE FUDGE SAUCE

- **1 package (15.4 ounces) chocolate fudge frosting mix**
- **2 tablespoons light corn syrup**
- **3 tablespoons butter or margarine**
- **⅔ cup milk**

Mix frosting mix (dry), corn syrup, butter and milk in saucepan. Cook, stirring frequently, until mixture boils. Boil 1 minute.

Substitution

For Chocolate Fudge Sauce: ¼ cup chocolate ice-cream topping.

VARIATIONS

■ *Chocolate Mint Shake:* Add ⅛ teaspoon peppermint extract.

■ *Chocolate Mocha Shake:* Add ½ teaspoon powdered instant coffee.

PINEAPPLE MILK SHAKE

Measure ¼ cup pineapple ice-cream topping and ¾ cup milk into blender. Cover; blend 2 seconds. Add 3 scoops vanilla ice cream; blend at low speed 5 seconds. (Or, use rotary beater.)

1 serving.

VARIATIONS

■ *Cherry Milk Shake:* Substitute cherry ice-cream topping for the pineapple ice-cream topping.

■ *Strawberry Milk Shake:* Substitute strawberry ice-cream topping for the pineapple ice-cream topping.

HOT CHOCOLATE MILK

Heat 1 quart chocolate-flavored milk over medium-low heat until small bubbles form around edge of pan. Beat with rotary beater until foamy.

6 servings (⅔ cup each).

CONTINENTAL COCOA

- **2 cups milk**
- **⅓ cup Chocolate Fudge Sauce (left)**
- **¼ teaspoon cinnamon**
- **3 or 4 large marshmallows**

Mix milk, Chocolate Fudge Sauce and cinnamon in saucepan. Heat through, stirring occasionally, but do not boil. Drop a marshmallow into each cup and pour hot cocoa over it.

3 or 4 servings (½ to ⅔ cup each).

COCOA-FLAVORED COFFEE

For each serving, stir ½ teaspoon cocoa into 1 cup hot coffee.

Soups

VEGETABLE CHEESE CHOWDER

- 1 package (10 ounces) frozen mixed vegetables
- 1 can (10¾ ounces) condensed cream of chicken soup
- 1 soup can milk
- 1 cup shredded Cheddar cheese (4 ounces)

Cook vegetables as directed on package; drain. Return to saucepan. Stir in soup and milk. Heat through, stirring occasionally. Sprinkle cheese on each serving.

4 servings (about 1 cup each).

CREAM OF CORN SOUP

- 1 can (10¾ ounces) condensed cream of chicken soup
- 1½ cups milk
- ½ cup mayonnaise
- 1 can (16 ounces) whole kernel corn
  Chopped pimiento
  Snipped parsley

Heat soup, milk, mayonnaise and corn, stirring occasionally. Garnish with pimiento and parsley.

5 servings (1 cup each).

SHRIMP BISQUE

Pictured on page 101.

- 1 can (10¾ ounces) condensed tomato soup
- 1 can (10¾ ounces) condensed cream of shrimp soup
- 2 cups milk
- 1 can (4½ ounces) broken shrimp, rinsed and drained

Heat tomato soup, shrimp soup and milk, stirring occasionally. Stir in shrimp; heat through.

4 servings (1 cup each).

HERBED SOUPS

For a new flavor in soup, heat one of the following combinations:

- 1 can (10¾ ounces) condensed chicken noodle soup
- 1 can (10¾ ounces) condensed chicken with rice soup
- 1 soup can water
- ½ teaspoon majoram

- 1 can (10¾ ounces) condensed tomato soup
- 1 soup can milk
- ¼ teaspoon cloves

- 1 can (10¾ ounces) condensed cream of chicken soup
- 1 soup can water
- ¼ teaspoon curry powder

- 1 can (11½ ounces) condensed green pea soup
- 1 soup can water or milk
- ¼ teaspoon chili powder

3 servings (about ¾ cup each).

QUICK SOUP COMBOS

Create a new soup treat by combining and heating old favorites. For example:

- 1 can (10¾ ounces) condensed beef noodle soup
- 1 can (10¾ ounces) condensed tomato soup
- 1 soup can water
- 1 soup can milk

- 1 can (11 ounces) condensed Cheddar cheese soup
- 1 can (10¾ ounces) condensed tomato soup
- 1 soup can water
- 1 soup can milk

- 1 envelope (1¾ ounces) chicken noodle soup mix, prepared
- 1 envelope (about 1½ ounces) onion soup mix, prepared

- 1 can (10¾ ounces) condensed vegetable soup
- 1 can (11½ ounces) bean with bacon soup
- 2 soup cans water

5 servings (1 cup each).

CLAM AND TOMATO BISQUE

1 can (7 to 8 ounces) minced clams
1 can (10¾ ounces) condensed
   tomato soup
1 soup can water
1 teaspoon salt
⅛ teaspoon pepper
1 teaspoon lemon juice

Heat clams (with liquor) and remaining ingredients to boiling. Reduce heat; simmer 5 minutes.

4 servings (about ¾ cup each).

CLAM-POTATO CHOWDER

1 package (5.5 ounces) scalloped potatoes
1 can (7 to 8 ounces) minced clams,
   drained (reserve liquor)
2½ cups milk
1 tablespoon butter or margarine

In large saucepan, heat potato slices, sauce mix, amounts of water and milk called for on package and clam liquor to boiling, stirring occasionally. Reduce heat.

Cover tightly; simmer about 25 minutes or until potatoes are tender, stirring occasionally. Stir in clams, 2½ cups milk and the butter; heat through.

6 servings (about 1 cup each).

VARIATIONS

■ *Clam-Corn Chowder:* Stir in 1 can (8 ounces) whole kernel corn, drained, with the clams.

■ *Lobster Chowder:* Omit clams and liquor; stir in 1 can (5 ounces) lobster, drained and broken into small pieces, with the milk and butter.

SHERRIED MADRILENE

2 cans (13 ounces each) clear madrilene
2 cans (13 ounces each) red madrilene
½ cup sherry

Heat madrilenes to boiling. Remove from heat; stir in wine. Serve immediately.

5 servings (about ¾ cup each).

CREAMY POTATO SOUP

2 tablespoons butter or margarine
2 tablespoons finely chopped onion
1½ teaspoons salt
¼ teaspoon celery salt
⅛ teaspoon pepper
3½ cups milk
1⅓ cups instant mashed potatoes
   Paprika
   Snipped parsley

In medium saucepan, heat butter, onion, salt, celery salt, pepper and milk *just* to boiling. Stir in mashed potatoes (dry); continue cooking until smooth, stirring constantly. Garnish with paprika and parsley.

4 servings (1 cup each).

Substitution

For fresh onion: 1 tablespoon instant minced onion.

SOUTH-OF-THE-BORDER BEAN SOUP

1 can (11½ ounces) condensed bean and
   bacon soup
1 can (10¾ ounces) condensed
   tomato soup
1 can (10½ ounces) chili without beans
1 soup can water
⅛ to ¼ teaspoon garlic powder
   Corn chips

Heat all ingredients except corn chips to boiling. Garnish soup with corn chips.

5 servings (1 cup each).

Sandwiches

INDIVIDUAL SUBMARINE SANDWICHES

Pictured on page 101.

- 4 loaves French bread, each 6 inches long
  Soft butter or margarine
- 4 lettuce leaves
- 2 to 3 tablespoons Italian salad dressing
- 4 slices salami
- 4 slices American cheese
- 4 slices boiled ham
- 4 slices Provolone cheese
- 4 to 8 slices tomato
  Thin slices onion
- 4 endive leaves

Cut loaves in half horizontally. Spread cut sides with butter. Dip lettuce leaves into salad dressing. On bottom halves of loaves, layer lettuce, salami, American cheese, ham, Provolone cheese, tomato and onion slices. Dip endive into remaining salad dressing; place on onion slices and top with remaining halves of loaves. Secure with wooden picks.

4 sandwiches.

CONEY ISLAND HOT DOGS

- 1 can (15 ounces) chili with beans
- 1 can (6 ounces) tomato paste
- ¼ cup chopped green pepper
- ¼ cup chopped onion
- 1 teaspoon prepared mustard
- ½ teaspoon salt
- ½ teaspoon chili powder
- 8 to 10 frankfurters
- 8 to 10 frankfurter buns, buttered

In saucepan, mix all ingredients except frankfurters and buns. Heat to boiling. Reduce heat; simmer uncovered 10 minutes. Drop frankfurters into boiling water; reduce heat. Cover tightly; simmer 5 to 8 minutes. Toast buns. Serve frankfurters in buns; top frankfurters with chili mixture.

8 to 10 sandwiches.

GRILLED REUBEN SANDWICHES

- ⅓ cup mayonnaise or salad dressing
- 1 tablespoon chili sauce
- 12 slices rye bread, buttered
- ½ pound sliced Swiss cheese
- ½ pound sliced cooked beef corned brisket
- 1 can (16 ounces) sauerkraut, drained
  Soft butter or margarine

Mix mayonnaise and chili sauce; spread on 6 bread slices. Top with cheese slices, corned brisket, sauerkraut and remaining bread slices.

Butter outsides of sandwiches. Grill in skillet over low to moderate heat 5 to 7 minutes on each side or brown in sandwich grill 5 to 7 minutes.

6 sandwiches.

VARIATION

■ *Rachel Sandwiches:* Substitute 1½ cups coleslaw for the sauerkraut.

HASH AND CHEESE GRILL

Pictured on page 101.

- 1 can (16 ounces) roast beef hash
- ⅓ cup catsup
- ¾ teaspoon oregano
- 1 teaspoon parsley flakes
- 2 teaspoons instant minced onion
- 4 English muffins, split and buttered
- 8 slices American cheese, cut into strips

Mix hash, catsup, oregano, parsley flakes and onion; spread evenly on muffin halves. Top with cheese strips. Set oven control at broil and/or 550°. Broil 8 to 10 inches from heat until cheese melts and hash mixture is bubbly and hot.

8 sandwiches.

Substitutions

For parsley flakes: 1 tablespoon snipped parsley.
For instant onion: 2 tablespoons minced onion.

TOMATO SHORTCAKES

Pictured on page 101.

2⅓ cups buttermilk baking mix
3 tablespoons butter or margarine, melted
½ cup milk
6 slices bacon
1 can (11 ounces) condensed Cheddar cheese soup
⅓ cup milk
Soft butter
3 medium tomatoes, sliced

Heat oven to 400°. Mix baking mix, 3 tablespoons butter and ½ cup milk with fork until a soft dough forms. Knead 8 to 10 times on lightly floured cloth-covered board. Roll dough ½ inch thick. Cut with floured 3-inch cutter. Bake on ungreased baking sheet about 10 minutes.

Fry bacon until crisp; remove and drain. Heat soup and ⅓ cup milk over low heat, stirring frequently. Split warm shortcakes crosswise; spread with butter. Place tomato slices between layers and on top of each shortcake. Spoon hot cheese sauce onto shortcakes; garnish with bacon.

6 sandwiches.

DENVER SANDWICHES

¼ cup minced onion
¼ cup minced green pepper
2 tablespoons shortening (half butter)
4 eggs
½ cup minced cooked ham
¼ teaspoon salt
⅛ teaspoon pepper
8 slices bread or toast, buttered

In 10-inch skillet, cook and stir onion and green pepper in hot shortening until onion is tender. Beat eggs slightly; stir in ham, salt and pepper. Pour egg mixture into skillet. Cook over low heat *just* until set. Cut into 4 wedges; turn. Brown slightly. Serve between bread slices.

4 sandwiches.

Substitution

For ham: 1 can (2¼ ounces) deviled ham and ¼ teaspoon Worcestershire sauce.

TUNA BURGERS

1 can (6½ ounces) tuna, drained
1 cup chopped celery
½ cup diced American cheese
1 tablespoon instant minced onion
¼ teaspoon salt
⅛ teaspoon pepper
¼ cup mayonnaise or salad dressing
6 hamburger buns, split and buttered

Heat oven to 350°. Mix all ingredients except buns. Fill buns with tuna mixture. Place each sandwich on square of aluminum foil; fold foil over sandwich and seal securely. Place on baking sheet. Bake 20 minutes or until heated through.

6 sandwiches.

SPREAD-A-BURGER

1 can (10¾ ounces) condensed tomato soup
½ cup shredded Cheddar or American cheese
¼ cup chopped onion
2 teaspoons salt
1 teaspoon dry mustard
¼ teaspoon pepper
1 pound ground beef
8 hamburger buns, split and toasted
16 thin green pepper rings
Pimiento-stuffed olives, sliced

Heat oven to 350°. Mix soup, cheese, onion, salt, mustard and pepper. Stir in ground beef; spread evenly on bun halves, being careful to bring mixture to the edges.

Place eight of the bun halves on ungreased baking sheet. Bake 15 to 20 minutes or until meat is done. Set oven control at broil and/or 550°. Broil 6 to 8 inches from heat about 3 minutes or until brown. Repeat with remaining bun halves. Garnish with pepper rings and olive slices.

16 sandwiches.

Chicken and Macaroni Salad

Speedy Chicken and Shrimp with Asparagus

Lunch Main Dishes

CHICKEN AND MACARONI SALAD
1 cup uncooked elbow macaroni
1 cup diced cucumber
1½ cups cut-up cooked chicken
1 tablespoon grated onion
1 tablespoon snipped parsley
½ cup mayonnaise or salad dressing
½ teaspoon salt
¼ teaspoon pepper
4 cups bite-size pieces lettuce

Cook macaroni as directed on package; drain and rinse in cold water. Mix all ingredients except lettuce. Cover and refrigerate.

Just before serving, toss with lettuce. Garnish with parsleyed tomato wedges.

4 to 6 servings.

VARIATIONS

■ *Tuna or Turkey and Macaroni Salad:* Substitute 1 can (9¾ ounces) tuna, drained, or 1½ cups cut-up cooked turkey for the chicken.

SPEEDY CHICKEN AND SHRIMP
1 medium onion, chopped
1 can (8¼ ounces) pineapple chunks, drained and cut in half
3 to 4 tablespoons butter or margarine
2 cans (10½ ounces each) chicken à la king
1 can (4½ ounces) shrimp, rinsed and drained
2 tablespoons lemon juice
3 to 4 cups hot cooked rice
Imitation bacon chips

In large skillet, cook and stir onion and pineapple in butter until onion is tender. Stir in chicken à la king, shrimp and lemon juice; heat through. Serve on rice; sprinkle with chips.

4 to 6 servings.

CHOW MEIN CASSEROLE

1¼ cups boiling water
½ cup uncooked converted rice
½ teaspoon salt
1 pound ground beef
¾ cup chopped celery
3 tablespoons instant minced onion
1 can (10½ ounces) condensed chicken with rice soup
1 can (4 ounces) mushroom stems and pieces, drained
2 tablespoons soy sauce
1 tablespoon brown sugar
1 teaspoon butter or margarine

Heat oven to 350°. Mix water, rice and salt; cover. Cook and stir ground beef, celery and onion until meat is brown. Drain off fat.

Mix all ingredients. Pour into greased 2-quart casserole. Cover tightly; bake 30 minutes. Uncover and stir; bake 30 minutes longer.

4 or 5 servings.

FRANKFURTER CHOWDER

1 tablespoon butter or margarine
6 frankfurters, cut into ½-inch pieces
¼ cup chopped green pepper
2 tablespoons chopped onion
1 can (16 ounces) cream-style corn
3 dashes red pepper sauce

Melt butter in large skillet; cook and stir frankfurters, green pepper and onion over medium heat until brown. Stir in corn and pepper sauce; heat through.

4 to 6 servings.

WELSH RAREBIT

1 can (11 ounces) condensed Cheddar cheese soup
⅓ cup milk
¼ teaspoon dry mustard
¼ teaspoon Worcestershire sauce
Dash pepper
4 slices toast, buttered

Heat all ingredients except toast. Pour about ⅓ cup sauce on each slice of toast.

2 servings.

TUNA ON A SHOESTRING

1 can (6½ ounces) tuna, drained
1 cup shredded carrots
1 cup diced celery
¼ cup minced onion
¾ to 1 cup salad dressing or mayonnaise
1 can (4 ounces) shoestring potatoes

In large bowl, separate tuna into chunks. Add carrots, celery, onion and salad dressing; toss until tuna is well coated with dressing. Cover and chill.

Just before serving, fold in potatoes. Add a bright touch with parsley and carrot curls.

4 to 6 servings.

BEEF AND MUSHROOM SALAD

1½-pound sirloin steak, 1½ inches thick
1 jar (4½ ounces) sliced mushrooms, drained
1 medium green pepper, sliced into thin rings
⅓ cup red wine vinegar
¼ cup salad oil
1 teaspoon salt
½ teaspoon onion salt
½ teaspoon Worcestershire sauce
¼ teaspoon pepper
¼ teaspoon tarragon leaves
2 cloves garlic, crushed
Lettuce cups
Cherry tomatoes

Set oven control at broil and/or 550°. Place top of steak 3 to 4 inches from heat. Broil until medium, about 15 minutes on each side; cool.

Cut steak into ⅜-inch strips; arrange in baking dish, 13½ × 9 × 2 inches. Top meat with mushrooms and pepper rings. Mix vinegar, oil and seasonings; pour on meat and vegetables. Cover; refrigerate at least 3 hours, spooning marinade over vegetables occasionally.

With a slotted spoon, remove vegetables to lettuce cups. Arrange strips of meat beside vegetables; garnish with tomatoes.

4 servings.

PLANNING YOUR MEALS—

When you stop to think about it, every meal you serve says a good deal about you. It reflects your cooking know-how, of course. It also shows off your ability to manage money, your knowledge of nutrition, your imagination, your own good taste and that very special feeling you have for your family. To make sure that reflection is a pretty picture, take this little refresher course.

PLANNING AHEAD

. . . or how to coordinate three meals a day with ease and expertise. The first thing to do is organize —your thoughts and your menus.

Begin with the Basic Four. You're concerned about your family's health, of course; so safeguard it. Get the Basic Four Food Groups down pat, and plan your meals around them. Here's what you need, every day, for your full share of good nutrition.

Meats: 2 or more servings
(This group includes poultry, fish, eggs, dried beans or peas and peanut butter.)

Vegetables and Fruits: 4 or more servings
(Plan on serving one dark green or yellow vegetable every other day, one citrus fruit each day.)

Milk: 2 or more cups for adults;
3 or more for children and teen-agers.
(This group also includes cheese and ice cream.)

Breads and Cereals: 4 or more servings
(Make sure they're whole-grain, enriched, restored or fortified.)

Note: Don't forget fats, sweets and extra servings they provide additional food energy and other food values.

You can be flexible though. For example, those two servings of meat per day can be scheduled any way you like. If your family goes for hamburgers at breakfast—why not? If they won't drink fruit juice in the morning but they will buy it as a dinner appetizer—then switch. What matters most is that they get their quota of the Basic Four Foods each and every day.

Think Through the Menus. Plan them by the day or by the week, whichever is easier. Either way, try putting things down on paper. Then you can see at a glance how breakfast, lunch, dinner and in-between snacks balance out.

If you start your thinking with the main-meal meat, the high-powered protein food, the rest of the plan will fall right into line. Besides, you'll know better where you stand with the budget. And stop and think. Can you double up on the meat and plan for a repeat performance?

Then consider your side-dish strategy. Round out the meal with a vitamin-rich salad and/or colorful vegetables. Think about potatoes, noodles, honey breads. And keep things pretty—mix colors, contrast textures, vary shapes and sizes.

Give the same careful attention to your other meals. When it comes to breakfast, plan to do something different. For lunches that travel, be sure to tuck in some sweets—that's one way you can try to control the amounts. For snacktime, push the fruit and vegetable munches.

Point of emphasis: variety is the secret of success in the care and feeding of a family. Keep an eye out for the latest convenience foods. Use our recipes and suggestions to introduce new ideas, but experiment on your own, too.

Now take a look at the total picture. Did you get in enough meat? Enough milk? Do all the servings add up according to the Basic Four Food Groups? Good planning! Easy, too.

EXERCISING ECONOMY

. . . or how to stretch your minutes *and* your food dollars.

☐ Keep a running shopping list. Jot down items as you run low, or as they come to mind. When you're tempted to buy on impulse, ask yourself: "Do really need it? Will my family eat it?" Remember

THE GOOD AND EASY WAY

food that doesn't get eaten is money *and* nutrition down the drain.

☐ Check the food pages in your newspaper and shop for bargains. But if the bargain takes you across town, be aware that it costs you money to get there. On days when you plan to stock the freezer, it may be well worth the trip. Other days, convenience may count more.

☐ Follow a shopping route, in the order of your menu plot. Buy meat first, depending on the day's best buy. Then match up vegetables and salad items. Move on to desserts and snacks. See how well-plotted shopping aids well-balanced eating.

☐ Brush up on your arithmetic. Check out package sizes and the cost-per-serving; buy the one that's best for your needs—small, regular, even extra large. This is true for meat, too. The lower-priced bone-in cut may well end up costing more than the seemingly higher-priced boneless cut, which allows an extra serving.

☐ Follow the seasons for fruits and vegetables. You can tell when they're in season by the lower prices and the plentiful supply.

☐ Read and heed package directions. The manufacturers of convenience foods have tested their products exhaustively; they *know* which procedures will yield the best results. Look for new recipe ideas on the packages, too.

☐ Remember that time is money, and convenience foods may well save you both.

SERVING WITH STYLE

. . . or how to set the stage to double the pleasure of family meals.

Revamp the Routine. Everybody likes change—even in serving patterns. Sometimes serve from the kitchen, other times go family style. Or give Dad the honors with the head-of-the-table treatment. Buffet service lets youngsters learn to serve themselves—and it gives them a good excuse for not sitting still.

And here's a cagey way to make sure hot foods get eaten while they're still hot. Call the gang together for a just-before-dinner appetizer. Something simple will do—like tomato juice with carrot and celery sticks, or hot bouillon with crisp crackers.

Be Dashing with Dishes. Mix and match colors and textures. Red pottery plates with white china cups and saucers are fun. Match up one shade of green dishes with another. Or set out plates in a rainbow of colors. Soups and cereals can be served in mugs as well as bowls. Fruits and puddings look elegant in wine glasses.

Try a New Cut of Cloth. Switch from place mats to trays to a table runner to a conventional cloth in a gay color or splashy print. Think about a roll of gift-wrap paper, the narrow size, for slashing off a special-treat runner. Or use contact fabric for cutting out place mats in a pattern. Brighten the scene with colorful napkins—those great big paper ones as well as the fabrics.

Show Off with Work-savers. Serve from attractive triple-treat casseroles that go right from freezer to oven to table. Let everyone share in the cooking with do-it-at-the-table helpers such as electric skillets, chafing dishes and fondue pots. And remember those backstage aids that can mean so much to your good and easy plans: electric blenders, knives and can openers; nonstick finishes on just about anything and everything. Indeed, good equipment is a good investment.

Spruce Up with a Centerpiece. Pile shiny red apples in a pretty bowl. Pop limes into an apothecary jar. Tuck a bunch of parsley in a demitasse cup, or tiny cherry tomatoes in a straw basket. And for goodness' sake, show off that prized piece of kindergarten art right alongside.

Now you take it from here. Use these ideas as starters, then dream up new ones of your own. You'll find dozens of ways to make do with what you have on hand and come up with imaginative, and very personal, treats for the family table. And that's what we call adding a dash of love to good and easy cooking.

FACTS ABOUT FREEZING—

	MEATS AND POULTRY	FISH AND SEAFOOD	STEWS, SAUCES AND CREAMED DISHES	EGGS (UNCOOKED)	
MAXIMUM STORAGE TIME	Red Meat: 4 months Corned Beef, Sausage: 2 weeks Poultry and Game: 2-3 months	3-4 months	3-4 months	9 months	
FREEZING TIPS	Uncooked: Trim off excess fat (to conserve space, remove bones). Do not salt before wrapping. Cooked: Leftover roasts and Swiss steak freeze satisfactorily for a short time.	Clean; wash, drain and wrap. For small fish, cover with water in leakproof container.	Do not overcook; cool quickly. (Fats tend to separate but will usually recombine.) Leave headspace in freezer container.	Stir eggs and egg yolk with a fork. Add 1 tablespoon sugar or corn syrup or 1/2 teaspoon salt per cup before freezing. For yolks, add 2 times the salt or sweetener recommended for whole eggs.	
THAWING AND REHEATING TIPS	Thaw wrapped uncooked or cooked meats in refrigerator. Uncooked meats may stand at room temperature *just* until defrosted and then be cooked immediately.	Thaw under running cold water in original wrap. Cook while still chilled. If only partially thawed, cook a little longer at a lower temperature.	Partially thaw at room temperature to prevent scorching. Heat in double boiler 30 to 40 minutes. Add liquid if necessary; keep stirring to a minimum.	Thaw in refrigerator. Or let stand at room temperature *just* until defrosted and then use immediately.	
NOTES	Freeze as soon as possible. Just about all meats freeze well. Do not freeze picnic hams, canned hams or other canned meats. Do not freeze fried foods.	Cooked shrimp can be frozen; shrimp cocktail and shrimp creole can also be frozen but no longer than 6 weeks.	Cool quickly by partially submerging the saucepan in large pan of ice and water. Potatoes do not freeze well; add when thawing. Keep spice level low.	Whites need no additions—put through a sieve for uniform texture.	

If you're interested in streamlining your cooking and serving chores without short-cutting flavor and variety, learn to use your freezer—or the freezer compartment of your refrigerator—to its full capacity. Cooking for the freezer is simply a matter of habit, and a very good habit at that. It can save you time. It can save you money. It can save you wear and tear. And these days, that's a lot of savings.

We've given you some specific freezing recommendations in the chart above, but here are some general guidelines for your freezer "savings bank":

1. Start with top-quality foods. Freezing will never make them any fresher or better than they were to begin with.

2. Remember that superior packaging and wrapping materials go a long way toward insuring a top-drawer product. Best materials include heavy-duty aluminum foil, heavy-weight plastic wrap and freezer bags or containers. These are all good because freezer wraps and containers should be airtight, moisture- and vapor-proof. They should also be convenient to use and occupy as little space as possible.

3. Wrap food securely in an airtight package—unless recipe directions indicate otherwise.

THE GOOD AND EASY WAY

RICE, BAKED BEANS AND PASTA DISHES	BREADS	CAKES AND CUPCAKES	COOKIES	PIE AND PASTRY
3 months	Quick Breads (biscuits, muffins, nut breads, waffles): 2-3 months Yeast Breads: 9 months	2-3 months	9-12 months	Baked Shells: 4 months Baked Pies: 4-6 months Unbaked Pies: 2-3 months Chiffon Pies: 1 month
Cook only partially; cool quickly. Freeze in casserole or in freezer container.	Bake before freezing. (Unbaked dough and batters lose some rising capacity.) Stack waffles but separate with wrap.	Bake and cool cakes before wrapping. Confectioners' sugar and fudge frostings freeze best. Boiled are difficult to store—freeze before wrapping. Or insert wooden picks in frosting to prevent wrapping from touching.	Arrange baked cookies in a sturdy box lined with plastic wrap or aluminum foil. Separate each layer with wrap or foil; seal. Package dough for drop cookies in an airtight container, aluminum foil or plastic wrap.	Baked Pies: Cool quickly; freeze, then wrap. Do not freeze custard, cream or meringue-topped pies.
Heat frozen food in covered saucepan (with small amount of butter in bottom) over medium heat. Or place frozen casserole in 350° oven until center is bubbly, about 45 minutes. (Add small amount of liquid if food seems dry.)	Quick Breads: Thaw in wrap at room temperature or warm in 325 to 350° oven. Yeast Breads: Thaw in wrap at room temperature. Or heat in 350° oven 20 to 25 minutes.	Thaw frosted cakes, loosely covered, in the refrigerator. Thaw unfrosted cakes in original wrap at room temperature 2 to 3 hours. Or place in 250 to 300° oven a short time, but watch closely.	Thaw baked cookies at room temperature for about 10 minutes. Thaw cookie dough until just soft enough to spoon or slice onto baking sheet.	Baked Pies: Thaw unwrapped at room temperature 2 to 4 hours. Or unwrap and let stand a short time, then place on lower shelf in 350° oven; heat just until warm. If using lightweight aluminum pie pans, place on baking sheet.
Casseroles of this type vary considerably and some loss of flavor may occur.	Heat frozen waffles in toaster. Overwrap bakery bread if it is to be stored longer than 3 months. A 1-pound loaf of bread thaws in about 3 hours.	Some frostings and fillings do not freeze well. The frostings change texture; fillings make the cake soggy.	Both cookie dough and baked cookies can be frozen.	Best to freeze baked pies—the bottom crust of an unbaked pie may absorb juices from filling and become soggy.

4. Before freezing cooked food, cool quickly.

5. Don't refreeze thawed foods.

6. Freeze in family-size packages or individual portions.

7. Clearly label each package (freezer tape and magic marker are good for this) with the contents, number of servings and expiration date. Rotate packages so the nearest-to-expiration-date foods are near the front.

8. Store food at 0° or lower (unless directions specify otherwise); the temperature will affect the quality of the food. In fact, it's a good idea to keep a freezer thermometer in the compartment to be sure the temperature's low enough.

Following are some estimated maximum storage times for other freezer-ready foods:

Food	Storage Time
Butter	6 months
Canapés	1 month
Candies	1 year
Cheese (small amounts)	6 months
Ice Cream	3 weeks
Vegetables	1 year

CARVING—THE GOOD AND EASY WAY

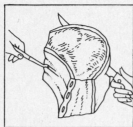

Beef Standing Rib Roast

■ Start with large side down. (If necessary, remove wedge-shaped slice from large end so roast will stand firmly.)

■ Insert fork firmly below first rib; cut horizontal slices from the outside of roast toward the rib side.

■ Cut several thin slices or one or two thick slices, if you prefer. Then cut down along inner side of rib bone. (Cut as close to the bone as possible.) As each slice is released, slide knife under it and lift to plate.

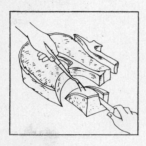

Beef Blade Pot-roast

■ Cut between muscles and around bones (bones are easily removed). Remove one section of pot-roast at a time.

■ Turn section so grain runs parallel to platter; carve across the grain. (Slices should be about 1/4 inch thick.)

Porterhouse Steak

■ Start with bone at carver's right. Cut closely around bone and remove.

■ Carve 1-inch-wide slices across the full width of steak. Carve thick steaks on the diagonal.

Pork Loin Roast

■ First remove backbone by cutting between rib ends and backbone.

■ With rib side toward carver, cut slices on each side of rib bones. (Every other slice will have a bone.)

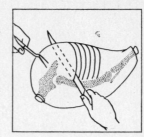

Whole Ham

■ Start with the fat side up and shank facing right; cut a few slices from the thin side. (The thin side will face carver if ham is a left leg and away from carver if ham is a right leg.)

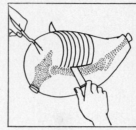

■ Turn ham to rest on cut side, where slices were removed. Make vertical slices down to bone. Then run knife horizontally along bone to release slices.

■ Or make only the first and last vertical slice and run knife along bone to release the section intact; then slice.

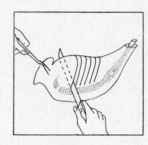

Leg of Lamb

■ With shank bone to carver's right, cut a few length-wise slices from thin side.

■ Turn to rest on cut side. Make slices down to bone.

■ Cut horizontally along bone to release slices (as for a whole ham, see above).

Turkey or Chicken

■ Start with legs at carver's right. Gently pull leg away from body and cut through joint between leg and body. Remove leg to another platter or board. Cut through leg between drumstick and thigh; slice meat parallel to the bone.

■ Make a deep horizontal cut into breast, just above wing. Insert fork firmly in top of breast; starting halfway up breast, carve thin slices down to the cut, working upward.